# The Fox Guide to Carp Rigs

The Fox Guide to Rigs

First Published in 2004 by Fox International, Fowler Road, Hainault Business Park, Hainault, Essex. IG6 3UT. United Kingdom
TEL:- +44 (0) 208 559 6500
FAX:- +44 (0) 208 501 1655
E Mail:- info@foxint.com
Web:- www.foxint.com

ISBN: 0-9549238-0-4

# Contents

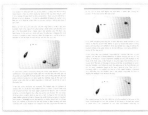

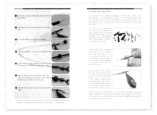

# Foreword

When the Fox consultants and I sat down to plan this book we all agreed on one thing very quickly: there's no such thing as the perfect rig. I don't believe it exists and nor do Adam Penning, Ian Chillcott, Andy Little or the author of this book Ken Townley. In fact, if you speak to any of the top-flight carp anglers they will almost certainly tell you they don't believe it either.

The aim of this book is not to try to blind you with rig science. You will not find details of any so-called magic rig in here. You won't find any airy-fairy diagrams of flight of fancy rigs that owe nothing whatsoever to practicality or efficiency, but more to the product of a bored afternoon with a bath full of water and a tackle box!

What you will find is no-nonsense advice on how to tie and when to use, some of today's most effective carp rigs. Like many aspects of carp fishing, rig choice is often a matter of 'horses for courses'. It is important to understand that a rig that might work a treat on one lake will be nothing like so effective on another. There are many factors that govern rig choice: The conditions, the way the carp might be feeding, the bait you are using; all are important factors that go towards determining if a rig will work on any given day.

With so much angling pressure now being brought to bear on carp water, rigs have acquired a status far above their worth. Some of the set ups we see here at Fox have to be seen to be believed, but for many anglers the notion of the infallible rig that will always catch fish has become a mystical Holy Grail and like the Holy Grail itself, the concept will always be flawed. I wish I had a pound for every person who has asked me, "Which rig catches you all your fish?" I'd be a very wealthy guy. The fact is that while most anglers favour one particular rig, they are not silly enough to think that their favourite rig is the be-all and end-all. They know they must be adaptable, water-to-water, and take every angling situation as it comes.

# Foreword cont.

One thing's for sure; choice of rig isn't rocket science. There are certain basic rules to be followed and these are outlined in this book. Follow these guidelines and it's a good bet that at least one of the rigs in the chapters that follow will turn up trumps for you. In this book we don't preach, we don't dictate. All we are trying to do is take the mystique out of rigs, leaving you, the reader with a clearer view of the part rigs play in the overall scheme of carp fishing. Knowing how to tie and when to use a certain rig is important, but it is just one part of the jigsaw.

Happy reading and tight lines.

Max Cottis,
Fox, Product Development Director.

# CHAPTER 1
# RIGS, WHERE DID IT ALL BEGIN?

Carp anglers are obsessed with rigs. If they blank it is likely that the first thing they'll blame is their rig. While laying the blame at the rigs door may be valid, it is not always the case. Bait, location, presentation, these may all contribute to the lack of action. However, it is vital to understand the basics of a good rig so that you can at least be certain that it is not your rig that is letting you down if you blank.

Before we start let's just look back into the days before modern rigs were invented. Back in the days of the "Carp Catcher's Club" boilies and particles were yet to be discovered. Bread, cheese, worm and potatoes were the main carp baits. Being, for the most part, fairly soft baits, the idea was to disguise the hook as much as possible to avert suspicion. When the angler got a run the strike was intended to pull the hook through the bait and into the carp's lip.

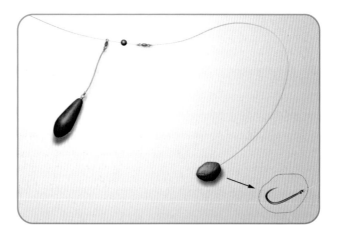

As carp fishing grew in popularity during the sixties baits became a bit more sophisticated. Now special paste baits ruled the roost but the end tackle was still set up the same way with the hook buried in the centre of the paste bait. The two main problems during this era were small fry nibbling away at the bait, and missed strikes when the run failed to produce a hook hold. Herald the arrival of the boiled bait!

In the late sixties the boilie was invented. This helped stop the problem of nuisance fish at a stroke but the problem of how to achieve a decent hook hold still remained and more and more anglers experienced aborted runs. Frustrated at being constantly thwarted by crafty carp spitting out the bait, the carp angler of the seventies turned to what we now term a bolt rig. Now, for the first time, the angler deliberately set out **not** to disguise the small hook by burying it in a big bait, but to make it blindingly obvious by mounting a smaller boiled bait on a larger hook. This method of mounting the bait was known as Side Hooking and when combined with a short hooklink and a heavier than usual lead, the idea was for the carp to hook itself against the lead when it bolted after feeling the presence of the hook and/or the hook point.

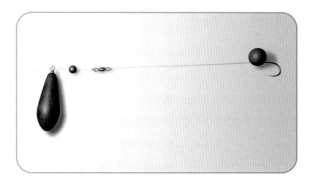

For a while everything was rosy but as more and more anglers turned to carp fishing so the fish became less willing to pick up bright little sweet-smelling boilies with any degree of confidence. What was needed was a way of making the hookbait behave in the same manner as the free offerings. Enter Lenny Middleton, saviour of the carp world!

It was Lenny who was primarily responsible for inventing the hair rig and together with the help of Kevin Maddocks set about changing the face of carp fishing, as we know it. Lenny's brainchild involved attaching the hookbait to the bend of the hook using a short length of very fine nylon line and thus the hair rig was born. The rest, as they say, is history as the hair revolutionised our sport. Now the hookbait could behave in much the same way as the free offerings and the carp were completely fooled by the way it behaved when they tested it. Previously when a carp sucked and blew at a bolt-rigged hookbait it behaved very differently from the freebies; now it was almost impossible for them to identify the hookbait from the free offerings.

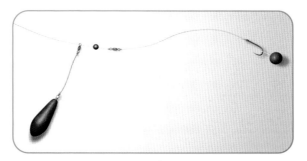

The original concept for the hair called for it to be attached to the bend of the hook. Good though this was, the position of the hook as the bait was sucked in meant that a fair proportion of carp were foul-hooked, especially by inexperienced anglers who tended to make the hair too long. The first significant change to the hair rig devised by Lenny and Kevin was to move the pivot point of the hair from the bend of the hook up to the eye. This was done in a number of ways, but the most common method was to use a piece of 2lb mono whipped to the shank of the hook beneath the knot.

With the hair attached like this, the force of the hookbait being expelled from the carp's mouth when the rig is ejected helps the point make its initial pinprick in the mouth, usually somewhere in the bottom lip. The thinking behind the change was to allow a distinct separation of the bait and the hook, thereby allowing the hook to fall downwards in the mouth of the fish.

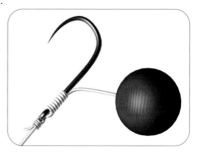

This repositioning of the hair from the bend to the eye of the hook not only led to fewer instances of fish being foul-hooked, it also provided the most heart stopping runs! Anglers who had been used to hitting tiny twitches and lifts of the bobbin found themselves being roused to single toners as the fish hit the lead and took off.

Both the power of the ejection and the mass of the bait contribute to any rig's effectiveness. As anyone who has seen carp feeding in a tank will tell you, they are able to take in considerable amounts of bottom detritus, ejecting what they can't eat with great force. Imagine this ejection force when it is brought to bear on the weight and mass of a 20mm hookbait and you can see why the separation of hook from hookbait is one of the prime requirements of a good rig.

The success rate brought about by this simple change in the position of the pivot point of the hair was the most significant development after the original idea and these days 95% of all carp rigs follow the principle of allowing the bait and the hook to separate in such a manner as to present the hook in a point-downward attitude on ejection.

The recent advent of more suitable, strong, long-shanked hooks such as the Fox Series 4 and Series 5 has brought about the rise in popularity of a whole new range of rigs that work on the principle of the hook behaving awkwardly in the mouth, as the longer shank is much

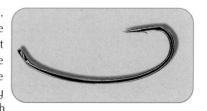

more likely to twist and turn within the mouth and it also tends to exit point-first.

Since the original concept was devised and then modified by Lenny, literally hundreds of permutations of the hair rig have been 'invented' and it has to be said that many have proved to be pale imitations of the original rigs. Nowadays, there are so many rigs about, it is small wonder the newcomer to the sport becomes totally confused by it all. Some rigs are so unnecessarily complicated that it has become a case of the carp angler fooling himself rather than the carp. It was for this reason that Fox International decided to publish "The Fox Guide to Carp Rigs". The aim of the book is to provide both newcomer and experienced angler alike with information on simple effective rigs: how and why they work, and when and where to use them.

The reason so much confusion surrounds the subject of rigs is because there are so many permutations being bandied about that nobody knows where to start. A common sight on many carp lakes these days is an angler working himself up into a state of frustration as blank hour follows blank hour. Time and again the rig comes off, only to be replaced by another all singing, all dancing rig, yet still he blanks. Most probably the blank has nothing to do with his rig but nevertheless the frantic search for the 'ultimate rig' continues.

Fox do not believe there is any such thing as the ultimate rig. What they **do** believe in is the concept that you can do more to eliminate indecision and doubt by following the abiding principles of meticulous attention to detail, backed up by simple, yet sound, tactical awareness and the use of the correct items of tackle for any given situation.

Fox have always been at the forefront of technology when it comes to carp rigs and accessories, but their over-riding principle is to keep things as simple as possible, always using the most basic rig to start with. There is seldom any need to go straight in with a high tech rig and after all, which rig do you turn to when eventually even the high tech one stops working? Far better to start simple and work your way up, rather than the other way around.

At this point, it might be a good idea to introduce you to a few basics before going into detail.

Many anglers make the mistake of thinking in terms of the hook/hair set-up in isolation, believing it to be the most important part of the rig. While it was true that in Lenny's day the hair rig was the be-all and end-all of the set-up, these days the modern carp angler needs to pay so much more attention to detail. Why? Because the carp in this country are now under more pressure than ever before and that pressure is growing daily as carp fishing becomes more and more popular.

It was Jim Gibbinson who coined the phrase "terminal tackle" when referring to this part of the modern carp set up. By this he encompassed not only the hair itself but also the hooklink, the swivel, the lead, the way the lead is attached and the section of tackle behind the lead. All these need to be considered as part of the overall picture rather than taking the hook and hair arrangement in isolation. Others refer to this critical section of end tackle as the Final Yard, the Business End or, as we like to call it, The End Zone.

You will soon discover as you work your way through this series of books, that a number of knots and accessories are used time and time again. One knot that forms the basis of a number of rigs is the Knotless Knot. This knot (properly called the Snood Knot or Snooding) has been around for donkey's years, being used in the 1800's by commercial line fishermen fishing for cod on the Grand Banks off Newfoundland. If it's good enough for them, it is certainly good enough for us! The Knotless Knot is one of the most basic, yet effective, ways to tie a hair rig and you will find that it crops up many times in the course of this series.

So in order to get you started let's just take a look at the Knotless Knot in more detail, examining how we tie the knot and how the Knotless Knot Rig (KK Rig) works with various hook patterns.

# THE KNOTLESS KNOT

1 First take your hooklink material – it can be tied using both nylon and braided hooklink materials – and tie a simple overhand loop in one end.

2 Mount your hookbait on the loop but if possible don't insert a boilie stop. Now thread the hook link material down through the eye of the hook.

3 Adjust the length of the hair so that the hookbait just clears the bend of the hook.

4 Hold the hook and the hookbait in the thumb and finger of one hand so that the hair length is secured. Now remove the hookbait. (Now you can see why you don't want the boilie stop.)

5 Now commence making the turns over the hook shank and the hair, trapping the hair against the shank. *Note well: ALWAYS start your turns from the side of the hook where it turns to form the eye. NEVER make them from the side of the hook where the end of the eye comes back to meet the shank as this may cut the hooklink under pressure.*

6 Make six to eight turns over the hair and the shank. (The number of turns depends of how long you want to make the flexible part of the hair and also at which position along the shank you want the hair to pivot from. A good starting point is to whip down to opposite the hook point).

7 Now take the tag end back down through the eye of the hook, all the time making sure that the turns do not unravel as you do so.

8 Finally, tighten the knot by pulling gradually on the tag end. (Moisten the knot with saliva whilst forming. As two surfaces rub together friction and heat is created. Moistening the knot in this manner reduces the damage to the line).

There are a couple of points to look at before we leave the details of the Knotless Knot. By threading the tag end of the hooklink down through the eye we create a much more aggressive angle of the hooklink material at the point where it leaves the eye. This tends to ensure the hook twists and turns in the mouth on ejection, thus finding a hook hold in the carp's mouth. This is particularly noticeable when using a hook with a down-turned eye.

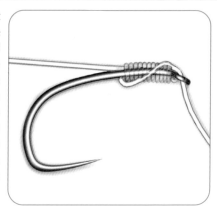

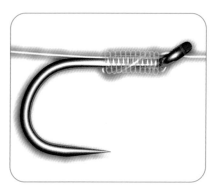

On the other hand when you are using a stiff rig, for instance, it is not always a good thing to have such a severe angle of the hooklink at the eye of the hook. That is where the Fox Stiff Rig Hook, the Series 6, comes into its own. This hook has an up-turned eye so when you tie the Knotless Knot using this pattern of hook, the nylon hooklink material comes away from the shank in a straight line.

Braid, being much more supple does not form such a sharp and severe angle at the eye, but this is no bad thing as braid's supple nature allows more freedom of movement of the hook and the hookbait. As they separate on ejection, the hook will automatically fall towards the bottom lip thanks to this suppleness. Straight-eyed hooks such as the Fox Series 3 pattern are particularly suited to braid and the Knotless Knot. With its pronounced in-turned point, the Series 3 is an instant hooker and the design of the point ensures that once the hook goes in, it stays in!

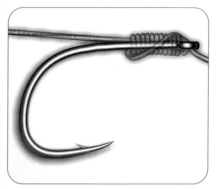

We urge you to pay particular attention to the length of the hair. If you position your hookbait correctly **before** the knot is tied, you can ensure that the hair will be the correct length afterwards. The correct length for your hair is so that the top of the bait just clears the bend of the hook. (Too long and the hair may pull the hook over on its back on ejection and the point will fail to lodge. Too short and the hookbait will hamper the action of the hook on ejection and again the hook point will be unable to get that all-important first pin-prick in the bottom lip).

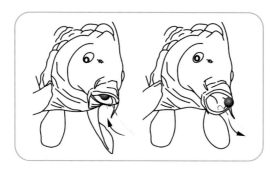

The number of turns you form varies depending on hook pattern and on rig style. On some rigs twenty or more turns are required. However, for the most part eight turns is sufficient. We recommend that you also make doubly sure of the knot by adding a dab or two of Fox Knot-Lok® to the turns. Be careful not to get any glue on the hair itself as the glue will stiffen the hair and affect its performance.

Before we close this chapter, let's take a look at the length of the hooklink. In general this needs to be between six and ten inches long. Shorter for Stiff Rigs using Illusion®, Rigidity or Slink, longer when braid or soft nylon is being used as a hooklink material. Of course, this is only a rule of thumb and as we progress we'll be looking at some rigs that are shorter than four inches or longer than eight.

Having tied your hook and hair set-up, you now need to attach the opposite end of the hooklink to a swivel. Nine times out of ten the best knot to use is the Grinner Knot and this is how you tie it.

## THE GRINNER KNOT

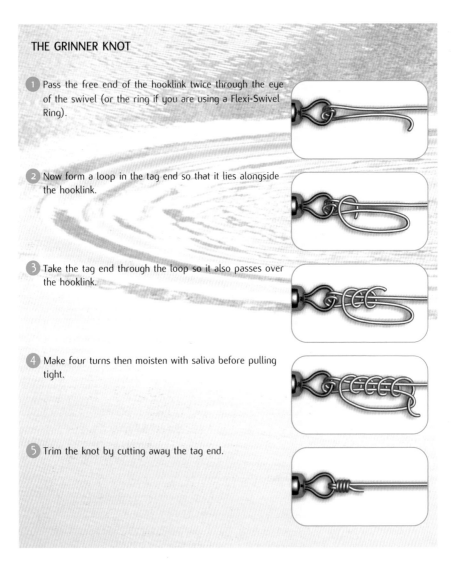

**1** Pass the free end of the hooklink twice through the eye of the swivel (or the ring if you are using a Flexi-Swivel Ring).

**2** Now form a loop in the tag end so that it lies alongside the hooklink.

**3** Take the tag end through the loop so it also passes over the hooklink.

**4** Make four turns then moisten with saliva before pulling tight.

**5** Trim the knot by cutting away the tag end.

Before we finish the chapter, there's one other key skill that will crop up throughout the book, Splicing Lead Core. Lead Core has become invaluable as a replacement for anti-tangle tube when fishing for wary carp as it ensures the line directly behind the rig lays flat on the lake bed, reducing the chances of spooking fish feeding close to your bait.

The Fox lead core has a camouflaged braided outer and comes in a choice of green or brown to blend in with the contours of the lake bed. A thin strip of lead runs through the centre ensuring the lead core is pinned to the bottom. It is supplied on a dispenser that fits the System Fox Box and is supplied with a miniature lip close splicing needle.

Over the past few years Lead Core has had a lot of bad press, because if used incorrectly it can be dangerous. However, follow these instructions and those in a later chapter on Lead Systems and Carp Safety and you can't go wrong. If after reading this you prefer not to splice lead core yourself, Fox produce Ready Made Lead Core leaders which can be purchased off-the-shelf.

To splice lead core you will need a spool of 45lb lead core, a splicing needle and a packet of Specialist or Flexi Ring swivels. (Some anglers prefer to secure the finished set-up with a dab of Knot-Lok glue. However, this is personal preference) The Fox dispensers come complete with a splicing needle designed specifically for use with all types of lead core.

# SPLICING LEAD CORE

1. Slide the braided outer sleeve of the lead core back to expose approximately 50mm of the lead inner, before cutting.

2. Find where the lead core finishes and insert the splicing needle as shown.

3. Feed the needle up through the centre for approximately 20mm and break back out of the braided outer before adding a swivel onto the braid.

4. Hook approximately 2 - 3mm of the tail under the hook on the needle.

5. Gently pull the braid back through itself as shown. It is helpful to dampen the tail first.

6. Once through, pull the tail tight, here we've used a Fox Tensioner Bar, trim the tag end then and add a spot of Knot-Lok Rig Glue to secure.

7. Once you've spliced the swivel to one end cut the lead core to length, approximately 45cm is about right. Repeat steps 1 to 5 but don't add a swivel, creating a loop in the end of the lead core.

Fox's commitment is to bring you the very best technical advances in rig technology and to give some background as to when and why they work. This book, the first of a series of three, brings that commitment to your doorstep. Each book will delve deeper and deeper into the world of carp fishing and in particular into the technical aspect of rigs and accessories in which the company sets so much store. In this book we will look at the following subjects:

1) **Assessing your requirements:** We shall explain how to discover as much as possible about your chosen swim, showing you how to use a marker float, Explorer Braid and Lead and how to judge the signals coming back to you from the lead as it moves across the bottom while you are feature finding. We shall also look at the step-by-step procedure for assessing which set-up is necessary on differing types of lake or river, paying particular attention to classifying

the water. Many lakes such as Drayton Reservoir in Daventry are comparatively easy to fish, as they are not heavily fished because the carp are small and plentiful. On lakes such as these, the fish physically need anglers' bait to thrive so action is just about guaranteed. In truth, these waters are more suited to the pole and pellet style of match fishing yet they are the ideal place for the beginner to get a feel for the kind specialised carp fishing that we

know today. On these lakes the carp are likely to be far less aware of the traps anglers set for them.

Then there are the moderately difficult waters such as Walthamstow 1 or the waters on the Waveney Valley Lakes complex. These are probably the most common type of carp lake and the carp receive the most intense angling pressure. These are not necessarily hard because the fish are super-intelligent, but because they are more lightly stocked.

Finally, there are the difficult lakes. These are not necessarily hard, because the fish are super-intelligent and have a deeply ingrained fear of anglers. Lakes such as Conningbrook where the head of carp is comparatively small yet the angling pressure is fairly heavy are classified as hard waters.

2) **Choosing a rig:** Once you have chosen your target water and assessed its classification you need to choose a rig. We shall look at the challenge presented by being able to read the water correctly as it is a fact that seldom do any two waters respond to the same tactics. Indeed, each lake, maybe each swim, calls for a complete assessment of what you are faced with and which rig will be best suited. We shall explain the choices facing you for each particular situation and explain why you should choose one rig over another and include a step-by-step guide on how to tie each one.

3) **A look at hookbaits:** We shall discuss hookbaits, looking at the full range from standard bottom baits, through neutrally balanced bottom baits and pop-ups. We shall again describe a basic rig for each type of hookbait and show you how to tie it.

**4) Concerning choice of lead:** As we said earlier, there is more to the business end than just the hook and the hair. Your choice of lead can be a crucial factor in the success or failure of a trip and knowing how and when to use a particular lead is vitally important. In this chapter we explain how to SAFELY use running lead and semi-fixed lead set ups.

**5) Snag Fishing:** Fishing in or around weed can be problematic if it's not approached in the correct manner. In Chapter 5, Frank Warwick covers the points he deems critical when Snag Fishing.

**6) Carp Care:** While not following in the general theme of a rig book, care of our carp once they are on the bank should be foremost in our thinking. Fox is totally committed to maintaining such wonderful fish in the best possible condition and we will be looking in detail at this crucial aspect of our sport.

All the rigs and methods described in the book have contributed to the success of the Fox consultants. Throughout the book you will find images and details of situations where the rigs described have proved successful.

Here Fox consultant and author, Ken Townley, is pictured with a 38lb Mirror taken on a Snowman Rig (described in more detail on pages 52 and 53) during a summer session.

# CHAPTER 2
# FEATURE FINDING

No two lakes are the same; indeed, no two **swims** are the same. Some may be better than others and some may only be productive under certain conditions. It follows therefore, that an ability to 'read' the water is very important as each swim needs to be assessed individually.

In an ideal word we would simply walk onto the lake, look around, see nobody else there and so have the pick of the swims. You wish! In reality it is more likely that you'll arrive 10 minutes after the weekend's masses have arrived to find yourself squeezed into a no-hoper of a swim. Might as well go home? Not a bit of it. While there are baits in the water there is **always** hope!

On every water there are certain areas where carp feed because they feel safe. In fact, many of the popular swims on a lake are popular only because they are not demanding and therefore easy to fish! Indeed, some of the most heavily fished swims often become carp-free zones in a matter of days as angling pressure, excessive noise or too much bait creates suspicion in the carps' mind. Carp like to feed where they feel safe and often the hard pressured swims are regarded as very **un**safe by the carp. So, even if you arrive to find the lake stitched up and all the popular swims taken, all is not lost. Get your thinking cap on and ask yourself, "If I were a carp, where would I go to feel safe?"

Let's just consider what might constitute a safe area from a carp's point of view. Well for a start, lack of bank-side disturbance is very important, as carp are very intolerant of the noise many anglers make, either as they set up, or when they are socialising on the bank. They are also very aware of your bait and in a popular swim the build-up of old, uneaten bait may be a cause of alarm. We would always advise you to use one of the 'active' baits as these break down quickly and do not leave a scary residue of rotting or uneaten baits in the swim.

Carp love to hang around, in or near snags; fallen trees always act like magnets to carp and carp anglers alike. Of course, you may be able to find them in the snags, may even be able to see them in there, but catching them can often be another matter. Similarly, overhanging trees and bushes provide cover and a feeling of safety and it is not unusual to see normally very cautious carp feeding on boilies apparently without any suspicion whatsoever under the protection offered by these features.

Islands and areas of an inaccessible treeline are also very attractive to carp as they are able to get away from noise and disturbance. However, you should always keep an open mind about such features as they attract a lot of attention from anglers and a constant bombardment of bait. If fish continually get caught from one spot it may eventually drive them away from the area as they come to view it as an "unsafe" area.

Finally, we have to consider weed beds. Carp simply adore weed, not only because it provides sanctuary and cover, but also because it usually holds food.

Whilst fishing in or around Snags, Weed Beds and Islands can be extremely productive we would never recommend that you fish so close that you stand no chance of extricating a hooked fish, should you hook one. In Chapter 6, Frank Warwick covers the rigs and tactics that you should employ when fishing close to snags to ensure success.

On most lakes you will find unpopular or lightly fished swims. There may be a good reason why this is so, but often it is simply the case that the swims are unpopular for other reasons. They may be regarded as no-hopers, or dead zones but remember that things can change very quickly on a pressured carp lake. Other reasons might include the fact that the swim is simply difficult to fish or too much of an effort (it happens!). They may be: too tight, too shallow, too deep, too hard to read, have too many features, be too far from the car park and so on. There are many reasons why these swims are unpopular but their very unpopularity can often make them productive as they represent safer areas as far as the carp are concerned.

According to many anglers we meet, one of the most tedious jobs in carp fishing is finding out what the lakebed is like in front of you. Well you may think it tedious, but we consider this to be one of the most important aspects of all and relish the challenge of finding new features.

The best method of finding out what lies below the surface is what we call "feature finding". This is done using a marker float and a lead that has been specially designed to find features.

The Fox Explorer leads are designed to transmit as much information as possible about the topography of a swim. The four 'fingers' will help you get a 'feel' of the bottom when casting around to find significant features in the swim. These may be weed beds, gravel bars, plateaux or silt and gravel patches. Each pack of Explorer Leads contains one standard lead and one with a wire stem. On the top of the picture is the standard lead, which is used over standard gravel bottoms; below it is the wire-stemmed version of the Explorer Feature Finding Lead which is useful for silty or weedy lakebeds or if you are experiencing difficulty in getting your marker float to rise to the surface.

You use the Explorer Lead in conjunction with a marker float. Fox produce two different Marker floats: the Carp Marker and Weed Marker. For general all-round use the Carp Marker is perfect as the shape is more aero dynamic and casts extremely well. Its slimline design means that it flies like an arrow with almost no air resistance at all yet there is enough built-in buoyancy to ensure it rises to the surface quickly and easily.

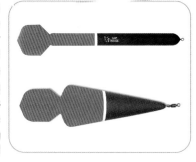

However, there are waters where bottom weed can cause the marker float to hang up in the weed and fail to rise to the surface. This is where the Weed Marker comes into its own as it is much more buoyant having a more bulky, conical shape to ensure it rises to the surface through even the thickest of weed.

A marker float is a vital piece of equipment for any serious carp angler. It allows you to find underwater features and, once located, the float can be left in place to mark the feature and act as a target for your cast and free offerings. However, once the marker float has done its job it is best to remove it from the swim as it can cause problems if left in place for the duration of the trip. You can easily find the feature again if you use the line clip on the reel spool. Feature finding can also be considerably improved by using a braided line on your reel. Fox have an inexpensive, yet highly effective braid that is purposely designed for feature finding. Fox Explorer Braid has a lot more feel compared to nylon and will help you discover the nature of the lake bed much more efficiently. The Explorer Braid's unique qualities transfer the

'feel' of the bottom back to the angler better than any other line. It is almost like feeling your way along the lakebed with your fingertips! A special coating allows the braid to slide freely through the Run Ring so the marker float can rise to the surface more easily.

Having the right equipment for feature finding is just the first step. Setting it up in the correct manner is vital. Here's how to set up the Fox Feature Finding system:

## FEATURE FINDING SET-UP

1. You will need Fox Explorer Braid, Explorer Leads, 30lb Slink, Run Ring and Bead and a Carp or Weed Marker float to set up the system correctly.

2. Take the 30lb Slink and attach it to the smaller eye off the Run Ring.

3. Cut the Slink to leave a section approximately 20cm long and tie to the wire loop in the Explorer lead. Adding this link keeps the float and run ring clear of any weed or obstructions that may be on the lake bed.

4. Pass the Explorer Marker Braid through the larger eye of the Run Ring and thread the Run Bead onto the braid. This will help to buffer the knot that you use to attach the marker float.

5. Now attach the Explorer braid to the tiny eye at the bottom of the marker float. The finished system should look like this.

Remember, for accurate depth measurements it is important that you take into account the length of the link on which the lead sits.

While we are looking at leads, marker braid and marker floats, it might be a good time to also look at the Fox Explorer Rod that completes the Fox Marker System.

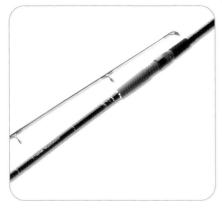

This twelve foot, carbon fibre rod has bundles of power in the middle and bottom 2/3 to allow marker floats and leads to be cast the maximum distance with the minimum of effort. In addition, the rod has been very cleverly constructed with blended carbon fibres and these are perfect for conveying the vital vibrations back through the blank when you are feature finding. This sensitivity is vital if you want to find features quickly and easily.

Because the rod is not intended as a fish-playing tool, it is has been designed to flex in the top one third of its length so that the marker flies straight and true to its target. This same action also provides visual and tactile information through the blank when the Explorer Lead is being dragged back across the bottom. The Explorer Rod was designed to be used with braided lines such as Explorer Braid, but you can also use it with nylon if you prefer. The final thing the Explorer Rod possesses is depth markers on the blank. This allows the exact depth to be established when paying off line from the spool of a reel.

Right! Now we are ready to start leading around to find the sort of features that might hold carp.

Stand facing the area you wish to search and cast out, feathering the lead down as it nears the water. You need to keep in contact with the lead as it sinks as you

can tell a great deal about the nature of the lakebed from the feel of the lead hitting the bottom. You will soon get a sixth sense of what the lead has landed on by the feel of the lead hitting the bottom. On gravel, for instance, you should feel a distinct thump as the lead touches down, whereas on mud or silt the touchdown will be more muted.

Point the rod tip in the direction of the line, and reel in a little until you are sure that the marker float is at the lakebed and touching the Run Bead. Now open the bale arm and carefully pull off a foot of line from the spool. For ultimate accuracy, place a mark on your rod a foot from the reel. Better still; use the Fox Explorer Rod as it has

a depth gauge running along the blank to allow accurate measurements.

Keep pulling off line until the float appears at the surface. As you do so, count the number of times you have pulled line from the reel. This will give you a number that can be translated into the lake depth in feet at that point. Compare the number of times you pull line from the reel to the previous search. More pulls and the lake is deeper, fewer pulls and it is shallower. This difference in depth will indicate a change in the contour of the lake bed indicating a gulley, a bar or a plateau. If you are looking for an accurate depth reading, remember to add the length of the tail in the marker set up on to the depth.

Reel in until you feel the lead and the marker float come together on the lake bed once more then slowly sweep the rod tip to one side so that the lead moves across the bottom. The rod tip will respond in one of several ways depending on the nature of the lakebed (more of which in a moment). Once you have moved the lead say six or seven feet, reel in, cast out and repeat the process of depth finding until you have searched the whole

area that interests you, or you can feature find right the way into your own margins if you like. It is also a very wise move if you take a notebook along with you and make a chart of the lakebed by noting down your findings each time you cast and retrieve.

Try to be methodical in your casting. For instance, start to the left of the area to be investigated and work your way to the right until the whole zone has been covered.

Once you have found a feature you think might be interesting, mark it by leaving your marker float in place, then cast a hookbait (or hookbaits) to the feature. Now spread your free offerings, groundbait or spodded pellets around the area near to your marker float. We'll come to a brilliant method for re-finding the feature with your hookbaits time and time again in a moment.

Finally, line up the marker float with a prominent feature on the opposite bank so you can cast in the same direction again. In the example below we chose the final tree in the cluster. DO NOT choose something that is liable to move during the session such as a Swan or other wildlife.

Now it's time to remove the marker. If you don't you can be sure a hooked carp will wind itself around the line and at best move the marker out of position, at worse, come off! (Another good reason for removing your marker is to hide the location of a hot underwater feature from prying eyes! Why should you do all the hard work only for some lazy bones to come along and clock your marker float showing the hot spot?) Before you wind in the marker float, locate the Explorer Braid in the clip on the spool.

Don't concern yourself that you will not be able to find the feature again. You will be able to find it time and time again thanks to the far bank marker and the line clip.

On a large water such as a gravel pit, you are likely to encounter variations to the make-up of the lakebed. For this reasons it is important to be able to read the indications coming to you through the Explorer Braid and the rod tip. In the next chapter we'll look at this in more detail.

# CHAPTER 3
# UNDERSTANDING THE
# LAKE BED

Once you've mastered the technique of feature finding and can calculate the depth at specific points, the next task is to try and build an image of the lake bed you're fishing. Unfortunately, this is a time consuming process and the larger the water you're fishing, the longer it's likely to take.

In some instances, it may be better to visit the venue after work or for short sessions with just a Marker rod, notepad and pen. It's amazing what you can find out in the space of a few hours without the distraction of casting out your carp rods. Another ideal time to spend time feature finding is during the close season, (if the water has one and access is allowed during this period). An added advantage is you can spend this time watching for fish, which will give you a better idea of the routes they patrol and potential fishing hot spots.

Whilst all of the above is time consuming, speak to any top angler and they'll tell you it's essential. The larger and harder the water you fish the more essential it is. There are no short cuts to success and time spent finding out about the contours of the water you fish and observing the movement of the carp in it, will pay dividends once you start fishing.

Fox consultant, Ronny De Groote, is pictured right with a 25kg Mirror caught from a water in his native Belgium: a big pit approximately 25 acres in size with very few fish. In the first year that Ronny fished the water he didn't catch a single carp. However, during this time he spent a lot of time feature finding and observing the water. When Ronny returned to the water the following year, the sun had been shining for the whole week prior to his visit and instinct told him the fish would be feeding in the shallower water at the top end of the lake. Ronny positioned his baits at the bottom of a drop

off that he had found using his feature finding set up, where the water went from 3ft to 5ft. Within two hours he had a run from this 25kg/50lb fish. Just for good measure Ronny returned 5 days later and caught the same fish from almost the same spot. The moral is: time spent feature finding is never wasted.

On waters such as Gravel Pits you are likely to encounter a huge number of variations in the composition of the lakebed. The illustration below shows the sort of thing you are likely to find on many gravel pits: lots of undulation and mud, silt gravel, plateaux and weed. Therefore, it is important to be able to read the transmissions coming to you through the Explorer Rod and Braid.

After casting the marker set-up, and letting the float rise to the surface, it is time to retrieve the lead. The key here is to go steadily. Wind down until you feel the float reach the lead.

Standing with the rod parallel to the bank there are now two options. With the rod slightly flexed, pull on the lead and feel for the transmissions as the lead bounces along the bottom. In mud, silt or other heavy ground the Explorer lead can become buried. In this instance, it may be necessary to combine pulling on the lead with a turn of the reel to get the lead moving.

For the rest of the chapter we will concentrate on the behaviour of the rod tip and what this tells you about the composition of the lake bed and look at some rigs we can use.

### Gravel & Stones

The rod tip jerks positively, vibrating over and over again as the lead covers the bottom: This indicates that you are pulling the lead across gravel or stones, a hard

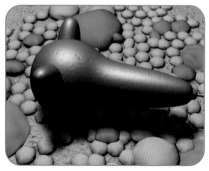

lake bed that makes for easy presentation. Carp like to feed in and among the small stones that make up a gravel patch. Gravel hosts a huge amount of natural food such as shrimps, freshwater snails and, most important of all, small freshwater mussels.

Gravel poses quite a few problems as far as presentation is concerned. Pop-ups certainly help to keep the hook point away from the bottom, reducing the chances of it becoming damaged on stones, rocks and gravel, but on some of the pressure waters a pop-up sticks out like a sore thumb to carp that have learnt that any bait that sits an inch or two off the bottom is suspect. On the other hand, a standard bottom bait will draw the hook down to the lakebed where the point is at risk. A good rig in this situation is the Snowman Rig, and we'll look at this in more detail in the next chapter. However, an effective alternative to the Snowman is the Snare Rig.

Snare is a slow sinking braid with a very high tensile strength and excellent abrasion resistance. These properties make it ideal for fishing over gravel. It is also stiffer than most braids on the market which helps prevent tangles and aids the delicate, yet robust presentation necessary, when you are fishing over a rough bottom. We have found that Snare lends itself very nicely to long shank hooks so here is how to tie the Snare Rig.

### SNARE RIG

**1** You will need a Fox Series 4 size 6 hook, 20lb Snare, Size 7 Swivels and 0.5mm-1.5mm Shrink Tube.

**2** Take a 30cm length of Snare and tie a boilie loop in one end.

3. Attach an ordinary bottom bait to the loop and position the boilie stop.

4. Position the boilie so that it clears the bend of the hook by 1cm.

5. Thread the end of the Snare down through the eye of the hook, then bring it back and make 15-18 turns of the braid over the shank to form a Knotless Knot. You need to bring the whipping along the shank to a point midway between the barb and the eye.

6. Take a 50mm section of the 1.5-0.5mm Shrink tube and thread it onto the Snare before tying the hook length to a swivel.

7. Position the Shrink Tube over the eye of the swivel to which the Snare is tied then apply steam to the Shrink tube.*

8. Thread a 0.5m section of 0.75mm Gravel Brown Barbuster Armoured Tube onto the mainline. Add a 4oz Flat Pear Bomb which is the best lead shape for holding on bars and gravel. Finally attach the hooklink to your reel line via the swivel.

*This is a dangerous operation and forceps should be used to hold the shrink tube in position in all instances. Children under the age of 16 should not attempt this step unless supervised by an adult.

9. Secure the Barbuster tube in the tail rubber. This gives a nice streamlined profile to the lead/tubing set-up.

10. This completes the Snare Rig and the rest of the End Zone. However, we haven't got to the sneaky bit yet! With an 8mm Boilie Punch cut a section of boilie from the centre of the hookbait. (It's a good idea only to go about half of the way through rather than right through the bait.)

11. Now take some appropriately coloured 8mm Boilie Foam and insert a 'plug' of foam into the hole you have just drilled out using the punch. In this instance we've used yellow foam for illustrative purposes. Match the colour of the foam to the bait you are using when fishing.

12. Place the doctored hookbait on your lip close baiting needle, ensuring that you pass it through the bait and the foam insert, and position it on the boilie loop. Then add the boilie stop.

13. Finally test the rig in the margins. It should sink very, very slowly as the foam adds neutral buoyancy to the hookbait. If it sinks too fast, place a sliver of extra foam in the boilie loop along with the boilie stop. If the bait doesn't sink, rub a tiny dab of Supa Weight Tungsten Putty into the turns of Snare forming the knotless knot. This will ensure the hookbait sinks very slowly.

The advantages of this rig are clear. It is very tough throughout the End Zone so it will withstand the hard bottom superbly well. In addition, the hookbait sinks only very slowly, minimising the risk of damage to the hook point. If you are likely to have to pull back to find the gravel, it is a good idea to add a piece of High Riser Foam to the hook as this will keep the point clear of the gravel while you pull back.

### Gravel & Silt

The rod tip moves in a series of jerks, hard then soft, then hard again: This means that the lead is probably pulling across an undulating mixed lake bed comprising pockets of silt between harder patches of gravel. Here presentation can be more difficult as there is a big difference between presenting a bait in silt and on gravel. Silt can either be very productive or not productive at all, depending on its nature. Dark strong-smelling silt is

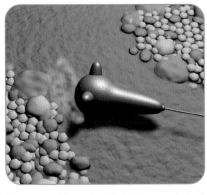

usually a waste of time whereas light, soft, non-smelling silt will hold a great deal of natural food like bloodworm and other invertebrates.

### Fine Gravel or Sandstone

The rod tip moves in a steady yet skittering manner: This probably indicates a clean lakebed comprising very fine gravel, tiny stones or sand. In this instance presentation is fairly easy and most of the rigs in this book can be used to good effect. A good starting point is the Snowman Rig described at the start of the next chapter.

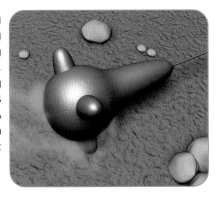

### Mud & Silt

The tip pulls round completely and seems reluctant to come free. When it does so it comes with a sudden release: The lead is probably buried in deep, soft silt and mud. Presentation can be very tricky here, as you need to know the depth of the silt in order to present a bait on top of it. However, get the right spot and presentation and it can be highly productive.

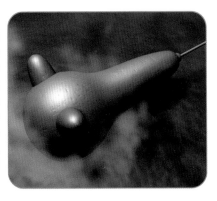

Silt can pose as many difficult challenges as gravel and a rig that presents the hookbait on top of the silt, rather than in it, is ideal. In the next chapter we will look in more detail at fishing in the silt using a Lead Core Helicopter Rig, but for the moment let's just consider a standard silt rig that will give perfect presentation over silt. For this rig we will use Fluorocarbon Line. This remarkable line is virtually invisible in water so the carp cannot see it. It has the added advantage of being amazingly supple and soft allowing the hookbait to behave in a far more natural manner.

## STANDARD SILT RIG

① To form the rig we need a size 6 Fox Series 1 hook, 15lb Fox Illusion Fluorocarbon Soft Link, 2mm Stainless Steel Rig Rings, Size 10 Flexi Swivel Rings, a Ready Made Lead Core Leader* and a Carp Safety Lead Clip.

② Cut a 30cm section of 15lb Illusion and tie a 2mm Rig Ring to one end.

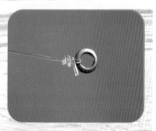

③ Thread the other end of the Illusion down through they eye of the hook. Position the Rig Ring so that it is opposite the barb of the hook. Form a Knotless Knot with 8-10 turns of Illusion.

④ Tie the other end of the Illusion to the swivel at the end of a Ready Made Lead Core Leader. Alternatively, splice a Flexi Ring Swivel to a length of 45lb lead core (see page 20 for more details).

5. Tie a buoyant pop-up hookbait to the Rig Ring using Bait Floss.

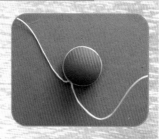

6. Counter balance the buoyancy of the pop-up with a suitable Kwik Change Pop-Up Weight positioned about 3-4cm from the eye of the hook.

7. Thread a Carp Safety Lead Clip onto the Lead Core Leader. before attaching the leader to your main line (see next chapter page 57/58 for details).

8. Finally, position your lead on the clip. Here we have used a Stubby Pear Carp Lead on the Safety Lead Clip.

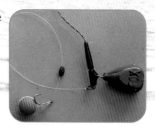

In practice, the flat-sided pendant lead will not sink into the silt as far as an in-line one; and the soft, comparatively long hooklink allows the counter-balanced pop up hook-bait to sit enticingly on top of the silt.

### Mud

Again, the rod tip seems hard to pull round but once free the lead skitters across the bottom before going solid again: This indicates the presence of weed. Where it is hard to pull the lead the bottom is shrouded in weed; where it is easy to move the lead the bottom is free of weed and this is where you need to place your hookbait to ensure it is in the clear when it comes to rest.

### Gravel Bars

The rod tip seems to go 'slack' as you pull back: the lead has landed on top of a plateau or gravel bar and when you move the rod tip the lead falls off the bar or plateau. You should re-cast to find the feature again; try casting around the area several times to discover the extent and depth of the feature. Presentation is likely to be fairly unproblematic as bars and plateaux are hard features. However, silt will collect at the foot of the bar,

especially on the side in the lee of the prevailing wind. Quite often this silt is full of natural food so it is a good spot to ambush carp as they patrol the gullies between the bars.

### Smooth Sand

The rod tip goes round into a smooth curve with no tell-tale movement as you move the lead across the bottom. The lead seems to glide across the bottom: You are fishing in a swimming pool! Either that or the lakebed is totally devoid of features. This may not be as bad as it sounds, for on lakes with smooth, featureless beds, the carp are likely to feed anywhere they find food. If that food is your bait,

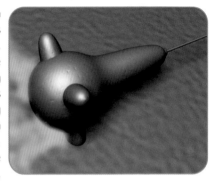

that is where they will feed. Presentation is easy, and not much tactical effort is needed to introduce bait and pull fish down onto it.

Once you have found a spot that looks as if it might be productive, you need to be able to re-cast your hookbaits to it time and time again, particularly in the dark. Remember, the marker rod is sorted out as you have placed the line in the reel clip and taken a visual sighting of a prominent feature from the far bank before removing the marker float. However, you don't really need to recast the marker float every time you catch a fish as you have got the far bank feature to aim at. But hang on! How do you know how far to cast in the features direction?

## CASTING CONSISTENT DISTANCES

1. Before you remove the marker float from the swim cast a rod carrying your hookbait so that it lands just beyond the marker.

2. Allow the bait to sink to the lakebed then pull back gently to ensure that your hookbait is lying on the feature marked by the marker float.

3. Next place the line in the clip on the spool. This means that when you recast you are going to hit the same spot every time. This is especially important at night, as you can imagine.

4. Have a couple of extra test casts just to make sure that the clip halts the cast in the right position to ensure that the bait is going to drop right on the spot.

5 Position the rod so that you can easily reach the rod tip.

6 Now take a 20cm length of Fox Magic Marker braid and tie a five turn Uni Knot (see diagram) around the reel line at the rod tip. This brightly coloured braid is critical when accurate casting and recasting is concerned. It will not slip or damage the line and its colour makes it easily visible in low light.

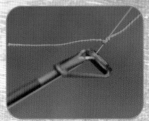

7 Now when you cast again towards the prominent far bank feature, as soon as you feel the knotted Magic Marker leave the spool and pass through the butt ring, you can start to feather the line and the rig will land in the right spot.

8 Finally, unclip the line and set the indicator...and don't forget to turn on the buzzer again.

There is no short cut to success and that is why we put such great emphasis on the correct way of feature finding. You will find that all our consultants, who include top anglers Max Cottis, Andy Little, Adam Penning and Ken Townley set great store in the amount of pre-fishing research they carry out. By knowing as much as possible about the lake-bed, you are then able to select the right rig for the job in hand.

## UNI KNOT

**1** Take an 80mm length of Magic Marker and lay it along-side the main line.

**2** Form a loop in the magic marker by bringing one end down behind the main-line.

**3** Pass the tag end of the magic marker through the loop four times.

**4** Moisten the knot with saliva before tightening. It is important when trimming the knot to leave each end at least 25mm long. This allows the knot to pass smoothly through the rod rings on the cast.

# CHAPTER 4
# RIGS THAT WILL GIVE
# YOU THE ADVANTAGE

Having chosen our swim and then found out as much as possible about the underwater terrain that is in front of you, it is now time to choose the set up that will give maximum advantage for all the hard work that went into your feature finding. In this chapter, we will examine a few different types of lake that you might come across in the course of a season and try to explain how to get the best out of each one.

## GRAVEL PITS.

Gravel pits, such as the one shown, are among the most popular type of venue, yet for the newcomer to the sport they are also some of the hardest to read, so let's start this chapter by going in at the deep end!

When you look over the smooth unruffled surface of a pit for the first time you can have no idea of the jigsaw of features that lie below. Back filling is the most commonly used process to form gravel pits and this process creates a series of long parallel bars. Where the digger turns or moves about the bottom, slopes and plateaux are created. In addition, the rich nature of most gravel pits means that natural vegetation grows freely and weed can often cause problems. Finding carp in a gravel pit can be a bit of a nightmare as they may be cruising down one lane between the bars while your hookbait is just a few meters away, separated from the carp by a great big bar!

The problems posed by gravel pits don't just include the bars and the other features. Often the layout of the sub-surface terrain creates currents and undertows that create silt pockets and where silt accumulates, that is where the carp go, as silt is a natural larder holding a wealth of the carp's everyday food.

Silt tends to build up where currents sweep the tops and sides of underwater features clean of debris. These undertows are created by surface currents resulting from wind action and you will always find silt in the lee of underwater bars and plateaux's, as well as in the shelter of islands and points. In addition, silt will collect on the lee shore (the shore towards which the prevailing wind blows) and fishing into the prevailing wind can often bring big rewards.

Food is almost always present in weedbeds – though some weeds are less productive than others – so it is always worth searching in and around the weediest areas, as fish just adore weed.

As you can see for yourself, fishing a big pit poses no end of problems, not least of which is the choice of rig. You see, before you can choose the right rig you have to make up your mind where you are going to fish. Are you looking for the silt or are you fishing on the tops or sides of a feature? On the other hand, maybe you are fishing through gaps in the weed. If so, do you know what the lakebed is like at the stems of the weed? Different weeds like different types of lakebed so again you need to make the right choice of rig.

One presentation that can be adapted from one type of bottom to another is the Snowman Rig. This very versatile presentation allows you to present a hookbait with delicate neutral buoyancy that will settle lightly on top of silt, bottom weed or gravel. It is therefore ideal as an all-purpose rig for gravel as you can use one rig for many different angling situations. As a starting point, the Snowman Rig cannot be beaten. It is easy to tie and can be used with confidence on most gravel pits.

As with all aspects of rig presentation, it is easy to become obsessed with the detail and the resulting rig can be unnecessarily complicated. Basically, there are only two or three versions of the original Snowman Rig but as we have discussed previously, it is always best to go in with as simple a rig as possible before moving on to more complicated versions. So let's start with the basic version, which usually proves perfectly capable of doing the job without any need for too many fiddly bits!

## THE SNOWMAN RIG

The main characteristic of the Snowman Rig is the fact that it uses two baits on the hair; an ordinary bottom bait and a pop-up. The principle behind the rig is that the weight of the bottom bait will counteract the buoyancy of the pop-up, thus creating a perfectly balanced bait that will sit lightly on the bottom without burying itself in weed or silt. Its neutral buoyancy also allows the rig to touch down lightly on top of hard gravel so the risk of damaging the hook point is greatly reduced.

To tie the rig you will need a Flexi Swivel ring, a size 4 Fox Series 1 hook and 20cm of 15lb or 25lb Delude Braid. Delude is probably one of the most versatile braids around as it lends itself to a wide variety of rigs. Its special construction means that it sinks very quickly and hugs the contours of the lakebed after sinking. Its extreme suppleness means that Delude is perfectly suited to all types of presentation, but particularly to those that call for a degree of counter balancing as is the case with the Snowman Rig.

## SNOWMAN RIG

**1** To tie the rig you will need a Flexi Swivel ring, a size 4 Fox Series 1 hook and 20cm of 15lb or 25lb Delude Braid.

**2** First need to place a Rubber Rig Stop on the hooklink. The Fox Rubber Rig Stops are supplied on a loop. To insert, simply thread the braid through the loop and slide the rig stop into position. After the rig stop is in place tie a small loop in the end of the Delude.

**3** Place the bottom bait on first and the pop-up just above it, and then insert the boilie stop. Next slide the rig stop along the hooklink so that it lies beneath the bottom bait, securing the two baits against the boilie stop and preventing the lower bait from slipping down to the hook shank. This ensures the rig

sits correctly in the water and also allows for a better hook hold.

**4** Now we form the Knotless Knot (You may find it easier to remove the hookbaits to do this but with practice you will soon get used to tying the KK with the bait(s) in place.) Remember to leave a gap between the bend of the hook and the rig stop. Once again the gap between the hook and rig stop is

vital to ensure the rig maintains its self-hooking properties. Finally, tie the other end of the Delude to the ring in a Flexi Swivel. You now have a perfectly balanced double hookbait that will catch all but the most wary of carp.

Tangles are of course, to be avoided at all costs and one of the best ways to stop tangles is to add a section of soluble foam to the hook so that the point is masked and the hookbait is trapped against the shank of the hook. Take a piece of Fox High Riser foam and dampen one side with saliva. Now fold the foam around the hook shank in such a way that the dampened surfaces come together so it covers the hook point

and keeps the hair in place against the shank during the cast. You will find that the foam will stick together easily as you press the saliva-moistened sides against each other.

A further advantage of using High Riser foam is that the buoyancy of the foam holds the hookbaits clear of the bottom for a few moments before melting. When the foam melts the hookbait is allowed to descend slowly to the bottom to sit lightly on top of the silt or the weed. It also allows you to pull back to find gravel or a bar without risking damage to the hook point as you do so. Finally, when it pops up to the surface the foam provides a visual target to indicate the area where your hookbait has touched down. You can immediately tell if the bait is in the correct spot by assessing the position of the foam in relation to your marker float (see previous chapter).

Here, Max Cottis, Fox Product Development and Marketing Director displays a 30lb Common caught on the Snowman Rig. The fish was part of a forty fish haul during a two-day session in early summer. "The Snowman Rig was particularly effective during this session, partly because of the lake bed but also due to the way the fish were feeding. Two weeks after this fish was caught the carp began spawning, so the fish were feeding confidently to pack on weight. The neutral balanced hook baits meant when fish sucked in the baits, the whole rig flew in and the carp were instantly hooked".

## RESERVOIRS AND NATURAL LAKES

Reservoirs can also be crammed full of underwater features. Damming a river valley and allowing the water to form a lake as it floods the land behind the dam is how most reservoirs are created. Obviously the underwater topography of the reservoir depends largely on what the land was like before it was flooded, but it is not unusual to find a wide variety of depths and contours.

You can see therefore, that it is not easy to classify all reservoirs under one banner as they can vary enormously. The one characteristic they mostly have in common is silt. By their very nature, reservoirs can get very silty and the older they are the deeper the silt can be.

The same can be true of natural lakes, estate lakes and some types of dug-out lakes. These too can become very silted up and where silt is a problem the rig we most recommend is a straightforward pop-up rig. This can either be fished with a standard set up comprising a pendant lead or an in-line lead. However, the best presentation for fishing in silt is the Lead Core Helicopter Rig fished with a pop-up hookbait.

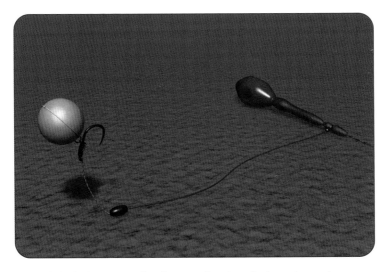

The use of the helicopter style of set up has largely been ignored over recent years in favour of the current popular fad for pendant leads held in a safety clip, and in-line leads. While there is absolutely nothing wrong with these, it is a shame that the helicopter is so out of fashion these days as it can be highly effective, especially when fishing in silty waters or at long range. The helicopter rig is the least likely set up to tangle in flight and due to the way it lies on the bottom the 'feel' of the End Zone up is very different to other set ups where wary carp are your target.

There is nothing new about the style of fishing that places the casting weight at the end of the reel line. Sea anglers have been using this principle for decades. Where the carp angler's set up differs is that the hooklink is intended to revolve around the main line during the cast. This ability to revolve gives the rig its name and its tangle-free qualities.

In practical terms the helicopter rig is a bolt rig, as the carp feels the resistance of the lead as it picks up the bait: This usually causes it to bolt. In deep silt the Lead Core Helicopter Rig can be used to place a hookbait on top of the silt. We'll see how later on.

Fox produce two ready-made helicopter 'systems': the Lead Core Helicopter Rigs and Barbuster Helicopter Rigs, plus a self-assembly Helicopter Safety Bead. We will deal here with the Lead Core rigs but the principles hold for both other systems.

First, choose the lead that will suit you best. If you are going for distance a Rangemaster Lead will be best, however, if you require the best possible bolt effect we suggest the Dumpy Multi-Bomb or, best of all, the Stubby Pear Lead.

You will notice a neat little Speed Link spliced into the business end of the Lead Core Helicopter Rig. This permits you to attach the lead of your choice with ease but it also means that you can change the shape and size of your lead whenever you wish.

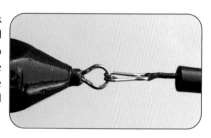

Having clipped on your lead, slide the Safety Sleeve down over the link and the loop in the lead. This protects the vulnerable splice that attaches the Speed Link to the Lead Core. Make sure that the upper part of the Helicopter System is made up of the Large Bored Helicopter Safety Bead. This has been specially designed with a large internal bore to permit it to slide freely over any knots in the set-up in the event of a break off.

Next, you need to tie the lead core to your main line. Again, we have made this easy for you by splicing in a small loop at the opposite end of the lead core so now you simply tie your main line to the loop. You can use the standard Grinner Knot to attach the reel line to the loop, but the method we recommend is via the loop-to-loop knot. While a standard overhand loop is fairly strong in all open water situations, it can cause a weakness in the line which may give in hook-and-hold situations or when trying to pull a hooked carp out of weed. The Rapala Knot is much stronger and more reliable. This is how to tie it:

## THE RAPALA KNOT

1. Form an ordinary over-hand knot about two to three inches from the end of your reel line. Pull it close but not completely tight.

2. Take the free end through the eye of the overhand knot. Pass the same free end through the eye of the over-hand knot.

3. Pass the free end over the main part of the line three or four times.

4. Take it back through the eye of the over-hand knot.

5. Then pass it back through the loop formed.

6. Tighten the knot by pulling on the free end and the main part of the hooklink at the same time. You will probably find it easier to do this by pulling on the free end.

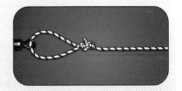

Once you've formed a loop in your main line, it's time to attach the Lead Core Helicopter Rig. In these pictures we've used orange monofilament for illustration purposes.

Take the loop in the monofilament and pass it through the loop in the lead core, then pass the rest of the Helicopter Bead through the loop in the reel line.

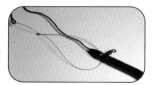

Finally, slide the two loops together so that they join neatly and tidily at the loop in the lead core.

An alternative method is to pass the free end through the loop in the end of the lead core at Step 2 above, then form the knot as described. The final step is to attach a hooklink and hair set up to the Helicopter Swivel. A simple yet very easy rig can be made using Mask or Insider, coated braids, to create a Combi Rig.

## COMBI-RIG

**1** To form the rig you will need a size 4 Fox series 2XS hook, a Kwik Change Pop-Up weight, a 2mm Stainless Steel Rig Ring, some coated braid and a Flexi Swivel Ring.

**2** Take a length of Mask (or Insider) and pass one end through the eye of the hook. Place the Rig Ring on the free end.

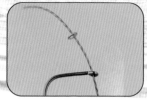

**3** Form a small loop against the shank.

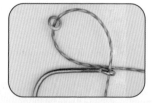

**4** Pass the Mask around the shank seven times.

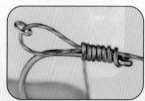

5 Form a Knotless Knot by passing the Mask back through the eye. Adjust the size of the loop by pulling on the tail of the loop ensuring the Rig Ring is level with the barb of the hook before trimming the free end.

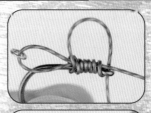

6 Adjust the size of the loop by pulling on the tail of the loop. Ensure the Rig Ring is level with the barb of the hook before trimming the free end.

7 Strip back the coating on the Mask for about 15-20mm before placing the correct sized Kwik Change Pop-Up weight on the line.

8 Attach your pop-up hookbait by tying it to the Rig Ring using Bait Floss.

You should find this set up presents the hookbait on top of all but the deepest silt without being pulled into it by the lead. However, you may find that the silt is so deep that not even this rig will allow the bait to rest on the top of it. In situations where the silt is two or more feet deep, you will need to adjust the rig accordingly by moving the Helicopter Bead along the lead core and securing it temporarily in place with PVA tape. This idea is based upon the principles outlined by Frank Warwick, whereby a short hooklink carrying one or two pop-ups is fished half-way along the lead core. No putty or other weight is used and the way the lead dives into the silt on the cast, together with the rest of the lead core resting on the lakebed, presents the hookbait just on top of the silt.

## SAND PITS AND MAN-MADE RESERVOIRS.

Having looked at two of the more difficult types of carp water, let's now turn our attention to a few slightly easier prospects, easier to read, that is, not necessarily easier to catch from. You need all the Tricks of The Trade if you want to catch consistently, so here are a few suggestions from the Fox Team which we hope will help you score on some of the most common types of carp water.

Many lakes are formed following the extraction of sand or clay. The process of extraction tends to leave behind a relatively featureless lakebed with maybe a few shallow gullies, the odd trough or two and, here and there a small bar or plateau where harder ground has been found whilst the excavation was under-way.

A similar underwater topography is formed in the case of man-made concrete-banked reservoirs. Again, the bed of the reservoir is likely to be bowl-shaped and relatively featureless.

On these types of lake presentation is not really a problem and while feature finding is just as vital as on any other type of water, you may well be faced with a flat, uninteresting bottom with apparently little or nothing to recommend it.

However, these types of lake are often very productive thanks to the slow but steady accumulation of fine silt and other debris. This builds up over the years to form a rich larder of natural food that the carp visit on a day-to-day basis. Find these natural feeding spots and you'll find the fish.

A very successful rig for this kind of carp water is the Swimmer Rig. This rig is very similar to the Combi Rig we have just looked at and is best used in conjunction with a critically balanced pop-up hookbait. The idea is to present the hookbait on the bottom rather than a few inches off it. The rig is tailor-made for our Illusion 24lb Stiff Link hooklink material as the resulting Stiff Swimmer Rig is virtually impossible for a carp to eject once the hook and the hookbait are inside the mouth.

## SWIMMER RIG

1. To tie the Stiff Swimmer Rig you will need a Fox Series 3 size 4 hook, a length of 24lb Illusion Fluorocarbon Stiff Link, a 2mm Stainless Steel Rig Ring, a Flexi Ring Swivel and a Kwik Change Pop-Up Weight.

2. First, tie the Rig Ring to one end of the Illusion.

3. Pass the other end through the eye of the hook.

4. Position the Rig Ring so that it is level with the barb of the hook. Form the Knotless Knot by making eight turns around the shank and then back through the eye.

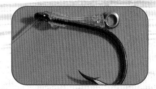

5. Tie the other end of the Illusion to the ring in the Flexi Swivel. (Please note: The length of the rig from the eye of the hook to the swivel should be no more than four inches).

6. Using bait floss, attach your pop-up hookbait to the Rig Ring.

7. Now place a Kwik Change Pop-Up weight on the line and position it one centimetre away from the eye of the hook. As this rig is designed to be critically-balanced, you should use the lightest weight possible in order to position the hook and the hookbait on the bottom.

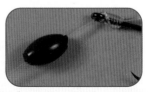

What happens is that when the carp picks up the hook-bait, its neutral buoyancy means that the hook jumps straight into the mouth. Then the short, stiff hooklink creates a very positive anti-eject effect as the fish tries to expel the bait. The result is that the hook finds a hold almost immediately just inside the lower lip or in the corner of the carp's mouth.

## SMALL DAY TICKET WATERS AND MAN-MADE LAKES.

Many anglers start carp fishing on well-stocked day ticket waters or specially created carp waters. One thing these waters usually have in common is a high stock level, but apart from this their underwater topography can be as different as chalk and cheese. While the high density of stock fish may make catching slightly easier, the successful angler will always take the time to explore the lakebed to search out underwater features, weedbeds and so on. In this respect, there is no difference between a low density inland sea like Wrasbury, for instance, and a small, well-stocked lake such as Willow Park. Other lakes may have a more reasonable stock level, enough fish to ensure most anglers catch a fish or two, but not so many that it is ridiculously easy. However, regardless of the type of lake the all-important research needs to be done first and we have looked at how to do this in previous chapters.

Another thing most of these waters have in common is that the carp rely, to a large extent, on anglers' baits to provide a large part of their daily food intake, as most lakes are not rich enough to support enough natural food to satisfy so many carp.

Having found out as much as possible about your swim, we now need to select a rig that is capable of fooling carp that are almost certainly heavily pressured and know that bait can spell danger, yet also know that they need to eat bait in order to flourish. It is very much a balancing act on the part of a carp. Do I eat that or don't I? It smells good, it looks good and I'm sure it will taste good, but can I risk it? Those are the metaphorical questions going through the carp's mind as it examines the hookbait. They are likely to regard any bait that looks or behaves differently from the norm with even greater suspicion, which is why pop-ups and critically balanced baits may not be as effective as you might imagine. In situations such as this, a bog standard bottom bait often does the trick.

While you might think the high stock level gives you a better than average chance of a take, this has to be tempered with the fact that carp are pretty cautious and will suss out any inferior rig. This rig is designed to take advantage of the carp's desire to eat the hookbait. As the fish will undoubtedly be cautious when it approaches the hookbait, it will be very tentative when it picks it up.

The rig we recommend is intended to give it no second chance as the hook and the hookbait separate immediately they enter the mouth, even if they are sucked in very tentatively. It is called the Drop-Down Rig and it is designed specifically

to be used with bottom baits. Indeed, it will only work with standard bottom baits and **must not** be used with pop-ups or even with critically balanced baits. We call it the Drop-Down Rig (The DD Rig for short) because when the fish picks up the hookbait and feels the hook, or the hooklink, it tries to eject the rig by forcing water out through its mouth and the bait is thrown forwards with great force towards the carp's lips. At this point the hook and the bait separate and the hook drops down onto the bottom of the mouth.

You can tie this rig with quite a number of our hooklink materials but it is perhaps best suited to one of our coated braids, for example Insider. This allows

you to form a small hinge or pivot close to the shrink tube, which protects the loop knot. Most of the Fox range of hooks can be used with the DD Rig but many anglers have found it works best with a hook with a straight point rather than an in-turned one. It should also have a slightly down-turned eye. The Series 1 is ideal for the DD Rig and for most waters we recommend a size 4. You will also need a Fox Lead Core Leader, a tail rubber, and, of course, a lead from the Carp Lead Range.

## DROP DOWN RIG

**1** Cut a 20-25cm piece of 25lb Insider and bring the end up through the eye of the size 4 Fox Series 1 hook.

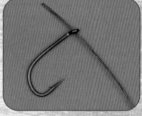

**2** Add a small 2mm Fox Stainless Steel Rig Ring. It is very important that you add after threading on the hook so that it sits above the eye of the hook.

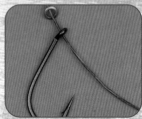

**3** Form an overhand loop in the hooklink and pass the hook and ring through the loop to capture the Rig Ring and the hook.

**4** Put a piece of Fox Shrink Tube over the knot and shrink it over steam or in hot water before stripping back an inch of the coating.*

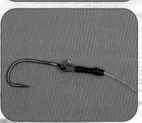

**5** Thread a small Fox Bait Band through the Rig Ring. This will hold the hook bait in place.

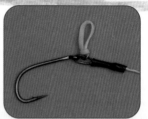

**6** Attach your hookbait and insert the boilie stop.

*This operation should be carried out using forceps and should not be attempted by anyone under the age of 16.

**7** Thread the tail rubber onto the hooklink with the pointed end towards the hook before tying the free end of the Insider to the swivel in the end of the Lead Core Leader. The length of the hooklink from the eye of the hook to the swivel should be no more than 10cm.

**8** Now push the tail rubber along the Insider and push it firmly over the swivel. This helps prevent tangles and ensures the hooklink falls away from the lead once the rig hits the bottom.

**9** Thread a Fox Carp Safety Lead Clip onto the lead core leader and attach the lead of your choice (We recommend a Stubby Pear.)

**10** Finally, attach your reel line to the loop in the other end of the Lead Core Leader.

**11** Before casting out, cover the point of the hook with a piece of High Riser foam to minimise the chance of tangles.

The DD Rig is virtually impossible to eject once the carp has the hook in its mouth and even the shyest of fish, once tempted to give the most cautious of sucks to the hookbait, will find itself hooked in the bottom lip.

# CHAPTER 5
# CARP SAFETY
# AND LEAD SYSTEMS

## LEADS

No look at rigs would be complete without considering the part that the lead plays in the End Zone so, in this chapter, we are going to look at the various leads that are available and discuss how they should be used and under what circumstances.

But first, we want to discuss carp safety and examine ways in which we can maximise the safety aspects of our fishing to ensure that our precious quarry is not put at risk by the use of dodgy set ups involving fixed leads.

One of the main problems with modern set ups is that they can become less safe when various bits and pieces are added to the End Zone. In a perfect world, we would all be able to fish the mainline right through to the hooklink swivel where a totally free running lead would be stopped by nothing more than a plastic bead. There would be no need for tubing, or lead core, or lead clips or abrasion leaders, or even shock leaders...in a perfect world!

Of course, we all know carp fishing's not like that and inevitably we will have to use some, or all of the above, from time-to-time. And that's where the problems can start unless you use your noddle. Often the inadvertent use of shock leaders, can turn what is a perfectly safe rig, when fished straight through, into an unsafe rig. Any knot, no matter how small and neat, can render the set up unsafe if careful attention is not paid to ensure that the lead or hooklink can pull over the knot in the event of a break.

Before we can show you how to eliminate possible problems from your set-up, we need to look at the causes. Rig tube is one of the best ways of eliminating tangles and it is probably the most widely used system in current use. For the most part it poses few problems, but there are several aspects of its use that need to be considered in order to make it as safe as possible.

Most tubing is designed to fit neatly and securely into a tapered sleeve called a Tail Rubber. This is attached to the back of an inline lead or Lead Safety Clip and it has the effect of streamlining the End Zone behind the lead, reducing the risk of tangles and making the whole set up neat and tidy.

Fox International design their End Zone systems with only one thing in mind, safety. However, even the safest accessory needs to be used in the proper way if it is to work as intended. Every item in the End Zone needs to be carefully considered to eliminate the possibility of the lead becoming hung up on the line in the event of a break.

Lets take the following hypothetical case. You are faced with a long cast to a distant island some 120m away. In order to make the distance you drop down to say 10lb mainline. However, you are going to need a heavy lead so you will also need a shock leader to absorb the power generated on the

cast. Consequently you attach a 4m length of 30lb Slink to your 10lb reel line. The fish in this lake are pretty cute and not fooled easily so you decide to use a braided hooklink. However, as this is prone to tangles you will need a length of fine bore Rig Tube to reduce the risk. Your favourite lead set up consists of a 4oz Inline Distance Torpedo lead with the 0.5mm Rig Tube secured in a tail rubber to streamline the whole End Zone. The hooklink swivel is jammed into the sleeve in the lead. You have deliberately used a large swivel to ensure that it is a tight fit in the lead, not easily displaced. Now, can you see the hazards in this set up?

You cast out. The lead flies straight and true to touch down just a foot or so from the island's margins. Perfect you think. You get a take, the fish hits weed and snags you up. You eventually pull for a break but all that comes back is the end of your 10lb reel line. So what are the consequences of your action?
This is what's still out there as you start to tackle up again.

1. A carp tethered in the weed that cannot free itself from the lead, as the swivel is jammed into the lead too tightly.

2. 4m of heavy duty line trailing behind the lead.

3. The shock leader knot where you joined the 10lb reel line and the 30lb Slink remains intact. This will prevent the lead from slipping off the line, assuming the carp manages to dislodge the lead from the swivel in the first place.

4. Assuming it does, can you imagine how potentially lethal the situation is now. The carp may be able to swim out of the weed but with the hook still in its mouth and the lead either hanging down from the hooklink swivel, or worse still, trailing 4m behind it, this fish is at terrible risk of becoming tethered.

OK, that's a hypothetical situation but it is one that may well be occurring at this moment, so let's try to see where we can reduce the risks somewhat.

What are the main areas of danger? They are the shock leader knot, the tail rubber and the tightly fitting swivel. OK, the shock leader knot is an inevitable part of the set up if you want to make the distance. But there is no reason for jamming the swivel so tightly into the lead that becomes almost impossible to dislodge. So how do we make this End Zone safer? It couldn't be easier! Simply remove the tail rubber and use a smaller swivel. Now the lead can detach from the hooklink swivel, slide along the tube and fall off the line at the point where the break occurred (usually at the shock leader knot).

Here are some safety points to consider:

1. The safest rig is one where the lead is free to run along the mainline or tubing, whether it is a pendant lead or an inline version.

2. You do not need a massive bolt effect to incite a run. The slight increase as the fish hits the lead and dislodges the hook-link swivel is enough to achieve an initial hook hold.

3. If you are fishing your reel line straight through to the hook-link swivel, then a tail rubber can be used safely as there isn't a knot behind the lead to impede it in the event of a break.

The most important consideration when using any lead that is attached to both tubing and a swivel, via any kind of bead, is that it's held in place by the lightest amount of pressure. To ensure this is the case perform the following test.

Hold the hooklink in your hand with the lead hanging down. Give the slightest upward jerk on the hooklink. The lead should detach itself from the swivel. If it doesn't, use a smaller swivel. This should ensure that the lead would pull free of the swivel as soon as that all-important jerk effect has set the hook.

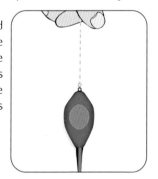

If you are using lead core, a shock leader or abrasion resistant leader you also need to ensure that the tail rubber will pass over the knot. Do not use a tail rubber if it appears to require a degree of effort to force it over the knot.

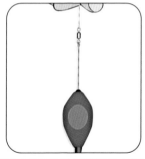

## LEADS

Generally speaking there are only two ways of fishing a lead and two ways of attaching it to the mainline. The two categories of lead are pendant leads and inline leads; while the two styles are free running and semi-fixed. The term "free running" is pretty self-explanatory, but semi-fixed needs a bit of an explanation.

When bolt rigs became widely used it was not unusual for anglers to attach the lead directly to the hooklink swivel using a clip. In these more enlightened days, anybody can see how dangerous this can be. In the event of a break off there is no way for the lead to fall free and the carp is attached to the lead until it either becomes tethered or the resulting mouth damage becomes so bad that the hook eventually falls out. Clearly, a totally unsatisfactory state of affairs.

On the other hand, nobody could deny that a fixed lead was remarkably effective, but there had to be a better way of 'fixing' the lead so it could become detached from the swivel. Thus the semi-fixed lead was born. A semi-fixed lead is attached to the swivel by a rubber or neoprene sleeve, or by some other soft material that grips the swivel lightly. Usually the bolt effect as the carp hits the lead is enough to dislodge the swivel and the carp can then get rid of the lead in the event of a break.

Let's look at the most common lead set ups.

### FREE RUNNING PENDANT LEADS.

We refer to any lead that hangs on the mainline, such as the Fox Carp leads, as a pendant lead.  There are two ways of fishing pendant leads, free running and semi-fixed. If you read the advice of many top anglers you may be surprised at how many suggest free running leads. This is largely regarded as 'old hat' in the modern era of carp fishing, but on the principle that what goes around comes around, many anglers are rediscovering the effectiveness of this style of fishing and totally free running leads have been the downfall of many of today's super carp. The illustration on the right shows a totally free running system, which also incorporates a length of rig tube to prevent tangles. It uses a Fox Carp Lead (in 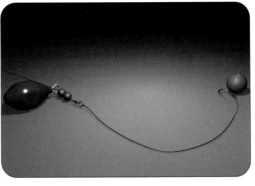 this case a Stubby Pear) and a Rubber Flexi Bead. How to set up a free running pendant lead follows over the page.

## FREE RUNNING PENDANT LEAD

**1** First thread a length of Rig Tube onto the end of the reel line.

**2** Now place the Carp Lead of your choice on the line.

**3** Thread the Rubber Flexi Bead onto the line.

**4** Gently feed the Rig Tube through the middle of the bead.

**5** Tie the reel line to the hooklink swivel then locate the tubing over the knot and superglue in place.

**6** Slide the Rubber Flexi bead down the Rig Tube until it rests against the swivel then add a dab of Knot-Lok glue to hold the bead in place.

**7** Allow the free running Carp Lead to sit against the bead.

In the event of a break the lead can easily slip free of the tubing and off the line altogether. This should make it impossible for the carp to tether itself.

## SEMI-FIXED PENDANT LEADS.

The term "semi-fixed" is somewhat misleading. True, the lead is 'fixed' to the swivel but only up to the point when a take occurs. The lead should then break away from the swivel so it can pull off the line in the event of a break. There are two excellent products in the Fox range that are tailor-made for creating semi-fixed leads.

The first are the Lead Safety Release Clips. These are designed to allow pendant leads to be fished semi fixed to the hooklink swivel. Available in two colours, black and brown, both designed to blend in seamlessly with lake beds.

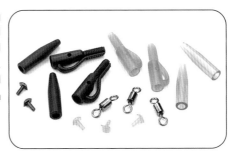

To use: simply thread the clip on to the main line before attaching the swivel supplied. If using lead core, ensure the swivel is spliced prior to threading the clip on to the line. Pull the swivel back in to the clip, which will cause the swivel to self-align, then the T bar can be inserted, locking it in place.

Once the swivel is locked in place, the lead can be positioned on the leg of the clip and the tail rubber pushed on to the clip securing it in place. Once complete the clip creates the ultimate safe bolt rig – the lead is held tightly but not so much so that it cannot pull out of the clip in the event of a break.

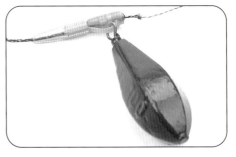

Another safety aspect of the Safety Lead Clip is that the lead itself is only held lightly in position. In the event of the lead becoming snagged in weed, under rocks or on a bar or plateau, the lead will become dislodged from the Clip and fall completely free of the End Zone.

A second method of creating a semi-fixed pendant lead is by using a Carp Safety Sleeve. These specially designed sleeves are ribbed allowing the Carp Lead of your choice to be positioned on the bead with varying degrees of release-pressure. They come with a set of Fox Run Rings and Speed Links to enable the lead to run

freely along the line once it has pulled free of the Safety Sleeve. We also offer a lead cored version that incorporates a pre-tied section of 45lb Lead Core with a swivel splicing to one end and a loop at the other.

To set up a Safety Sleeve follow these simple instructions. Place a Run Ring on the reel line, threading it through the larger hole in the Ring. Now thread on the Safety Sleeve and position the Run Ring at the desired position on the ribbed section of the Sleeve.

Next, clip the Lead of your choice to the small hole in the Run Ring using the Speed Link. The Fox ring in the Fox carp leads have been designed in such a way that the use of the Run Ring is unnecessary and can be fixed directly to the Carp Safety Sleeve.

Finally, ease the Safety Sleeve on to the hooklink swivel. The lead is now semi-fixed to the swivel but it will become dislodged when a predetermined amount of force is applied to it. You choose the amount by deciding whereabouts to position the lead on the Sleeve. It can be completely free running (position the lead at the pointed end of the Sleeve), or quite firmly fixed (position the lead on the blunt end of the Sleeve).

## FREE RUNNING INLINE LEADS.

In exactly the same way as free running pendant leads, free running inline leads are also not as widely used as they should be. This is a pity as the set up can be very effective when carp are picking up the hookbait very tentatively, feeling for the resistance or weight of the lead as they do so. It is another very safe set up as the lead is free to run along the Rig Tube, Barbuster or Lead Core. Obviously you don't want to incorporate a tail rubber into such a system as it will prevent the lead from running freely and the absence of the rubber ensures that the lead will pass over knots in the set up behind the lead. You can create a free running system by placing one or two Rubber Flexi beads on the line between the lead and the hooklink swivel.

## SEMI-FIXED INLINE LEADS.

Inline leads have become amazingly popular over the last few years and with good reason. They are probably the most tangle-proof designs and some experts' claim that they cast further than other styles of lead set ups. There are two points to look out for when you are using these types of lead. The first is the use of a Tail Rubber. These are used to streamline the area behind the lead and reduce tangles. Certainly they do this brilliantly, but pay attention if you are using a leader of any kind on your reel line. While the bore in the Fox Tail Rubber is large enough to slip over most knots used for joining leaders, always check to make sure the lead with the fitted tail rubber will pass over the joining knot with complete freedom. If the tail rubber snags on the knot and you have to force it over the knot, you must remove the tail rubber and fish without one. True, this may not look as neat and the risk of tangle may increase very slightly, but if there is any risk of the lead hanging up on a knot thanks to the tail rubber, you are going to have to make that sacrifice. It is vital to test that the tail rubber does indeed perform as it is supposed to; that it will pass over any up-line knots with ease. The only way to do this is to run the lead with the tail rubber attached over the knots. It should glide over with hardly any noticeable hesitation. If it stops at the knot and some effort is needed to force the lead over the knot, take off the tail rubber or learn how to use a smaller knot.

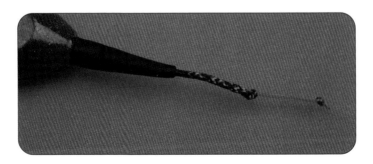

The second safety aspect to check is that the swivel at the end of the hooklink does not fit too tightly inside the sleeve in the inline lead. Yes, a degree of security is fine, but if you have to use a fair amount of force to pull the swivel free of the lead, then it is unlikely that a carp will be able to get rid of the lead and it may become tethered in weed or snags. Obviously, the fit must be tight enough to provide the bolt effect that inline systems are designed to impart, but the fit should not be so tight that the lead cannot be dislodged when tested in the way previously mentioned. Some leads on the market fit too

tightly over the swivel and can cause problems. However, the Fox Combi Lead system features a neoprene rubber grip sleeve, which prevents the lead from locking up on the swivel when fishing inline style, making it ultra-safe for carp. The bore is designed to grip swivels of the recommended size without allowing them to jam.

This is by far the best set up as the release of the swivel from the lead allows the line to travel through the eye of the lead and a much better indication at the rod will result. The set up turns from semi-fixed to free running as the fish hooks itself and then bolts.

There is a belief that hard pressured carp have learnt to use the weight of a semi-fixed heavy lead to rid themselves of the hook. When they feel the lead, instead of bolting off they remain, head down, sucking and blowing to try to get rid of the hook. They may even be using the physical weight of a semi-fixed heavy lead as a point around which they can pivot, allowing them to shed the hook. If the swivel fits only loosely in the lead and can pull free with only a little pressure, the set up then becomes a free running one and the lead is no longer able to be used in their favour.

## SEMI-FREE RUNNING LEADS.

You may think that a semi-fixed, free running lead is a contradiction in terms, but it is nothing new in fact. When we first used bolt rigs back in the 80's they were instantly successful due to the semi-fixed lead. However, it didn't take the carp long to start wising up to them. Now they picked up the bait much more cautiously, as if feeling for the weight of the lead. The logical step was to build in a degree of free movement into the set-up without losing the bolt effect and the way this was achieved was by using a backstop. With a backstop, the carp can pick up the hookbait without initially feeling the weight of the lead. Assuming the bait is safe the carp moves off, drawing the line through the lead until the lead hits the backstop. The sudden jerk as this happens creates a bolt effect and a run ensues. You can incorporate a backstop into both pendant and inline set ups. Here is how to set up a free running semi fixed pendant or inline lead.

## SEMI-FIXED LEADS

**1** First place a Rubber Flexi Bead onto the reel line. Now thread the reel line through a 0.5m section of 0.75mm Rig Tube.

**2** This is followed by the lead of your choice.

**3** Thread another Rubber Flexi Bead onto the line and gently feed the Rig Tube through the middle of the two beads securing the lead between them.

**4** Tie the reel line to the hooklink swivel and locate the tubing over the knot that joins the hooklink swivel and superglue in place.

**5** Slide the lower Rubber Flexi Bead down the Rig Tube until it rests against the hooklink swivel and add a dab of Knot-Lok glue to hold that Bead in place.

**6** Slide the upper Rubber Flexi Bead along the tube until it is positioned about 7-10cm behind the lead. **UNDER NO CIRCUMSTANCES SHOULD THIS BEAD BE GLUED.**

The resulting set up means the lead is now free to pass along the tubing between the two Rubber Flexi Beads. As the carp picks up the bait and moves off confidently, the lead runs along the tubing until it hits the upper bead; here its progress is momentarily halted and the bolt effect sets the hook. Result? Screaming buzzer!

## SIZE OF LEAD.

There are a couple of other aspects of choosing a lead to consider before we close this chapter, they are: size, type and shape of the lead.

Light lead or heavy? That is one of the most frequently asked questions we get. Unfortunately, the choice is not a matter of black and white. So much depends on the way the lake has been tackled in the past. We have already seen how changing trends create suspicion in carp and the recent trend for very light leads has brought home the fact that on many waters the days of the heavy lead might temporarily be numbered. (Temporarily, because it all come down to the 'goes around comes around' thing.)

Certain rigs depend on a heavy lead to make them work. Most anti-eject rigs fall into this category. There is also a school of thought that suggests that hook size and the weight of the lead are directly linked. The smaller the hook, the lighter the lead, they say. It is hard to draw hard and fast conclusions as to whether there is any weight in this argument, but it would be wrong to dismiss it out of hand.

Clearly, heavy weights are necessary when you are casting a long distance, but does the opposite invariably apply?

On smaller waters you can choose the weight of the lead and perhaps a lighter lead may be effective in reducing suspicion from pressured carp. Anti-eject rigs rely on the weight of the rig to work. A heavy lead puts tension on the hooklink and causes the initial hook hold that leads to hook penetration. Lighter leads will not work so well, but they come into their own when longer rigs are used. Unfortunately, that isn't the end of the story, as the question of the weight of the lead is inevitably linked to the way that lead is fished i.e. free running or semi-fixed. There are so many variables it would take another book just to examine all the permutations, so in the meantime, we will have to talk in general, rather than specific terms as there are no hard and fast rules; here are a few suggestions for you to consider.

1. If heavy leads are not called for to achieve the range, it might be worth trying leads as light as 1.5oz. These will be more difficult for the carp to detect if they are only toying with the hookbait.

2. If you are fishing in deep silt or weed you should consider using a lighter lead to reduce the chances of the hookbait getting pulled deep into the silt.

3. As a general rule of thumb, short hooklinks are best with heavy leads while longer, suppler braided hooklinks are better with lighter leads.

4. Semi-fixed, heavy leads may help prick a carp but they may also help it to shed the hook (as mentioned previously).

5. Free running leads, allow for a much better indication at the buzzer than semi-fixed leads.

6. Heavy leads are better for free running set ups than light ones.

7. Always be aware of what is going on around you, what others are using and whether they are catching more than their share. If they are it could be that they are using a radically different lead system.

### INLINE OR PENDANT.

Our carp fishing consultants are roughly divided 50/50 as far as their preference for inline or pendant leads is concerned. This reflects not only on the various types of water they fish, but also on the extremely complex nature regarding the choice of lead!

If your criteria is simply to achieve the best possible bolt effect; you cannot beat an inline lead. Though the shapes of the leads in the two Fox ranges are roughly the same, the inline Combi Leads create more effective bolt rigs than their counter parts in the Carp Leads. This is because all the weight of the lead is concentrated at the forward end, closest to the hook itself. In addition, pendant leads can pivot around the loop and this can give the carp a few centimetres of movement, possibly all it needs to rid itself of the hook.

The Combi Lead system (pictured below) comprises three shapes of lead: Dumpy Tri Bomb, Distance Torpedo and the Flat Pear Bomb — all of which are available in 8 sizes from 1.5oz to 5oz. Later in the chapter we'll talk about the type of situation each of the leads has been designed for. In addition, there are eight sizes of Combi Lead converter which combined, fit every type and size of lead in the range. The unique design allows any lead to be changed from an inline to pendant version (and vica versa) in seconds.

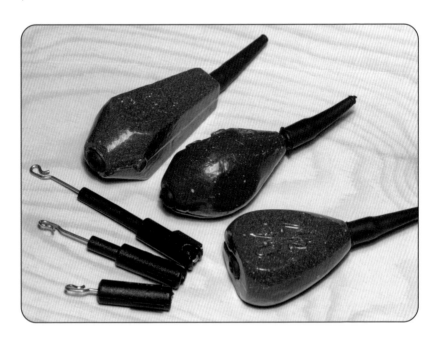

Converting the Combi Lead is easy. Simply take a Fox Combi Lead (in this illustration we've used a 3oz Flat Pear). Remove the neoprene sleeve, inner tube and tail rubber from the lead.

Now its time to transform the lead in to a pendant model. Select the correct size convertor: full details of which converters fit which leads are on the back of the packaging. For the 3oz Combi lead shown, a Size 1 Convertor was used.

Using a baiting needle, pull the Combi Lead Converter into the lead. When the swivel emerges the transformation is complete.

As the lead remains the same in all instances this halves the number of leads you have to carry around with you. There are three shape and eight sizes in the Combi Lead Range together with a vast range of converters and other accessories.

## SHAPE OF THE LEAD.

The final part of the jigsaw is the actual shape of the lead. In the past there was only one pattern of lead, the Arlesley Bomb, developed by Richard Walker. As a general jack-of-all-trades lead it was fine, but luckily for us there is plenty of choice regarding lead shape for varying angling situations and conditions.

The Carp Lead range can only be fished pendant or helicopter fashion, but again, there are the usual three shapes and eight sizes to choose from.

For distance casting choose the Distance Torpedo, from the Combi Lead range, or the Rangemaster distance lead from the Carp Lead range; pictured left and right respectively. These bullet-shaped bombs are designed to cut through the air giving longer, smoother casts. Their aerodynamic shape prevents the lead from wobbling in flight, adding yet more distance to the cast. Although great for distance, neither lead is ideally suited to presenting baits on slopes or in fast flowing water.

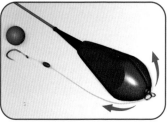

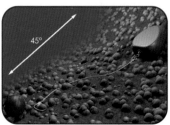

For holding on the sides of bars, plateau or marginal slopes choose the Flat Pear Bomb from the Combi Lead range, or the Stubby Pear from the Carp lead range. The flat nature of the front and back of these models gives a lead with a greater surface area than the respective size in the Torpedo or Multi Bomb design. This prevents them from rolling down slopes and the lead is more likely to grip on gravel or shingle as shown in the illustration. One draw back of these leads is that they don't cast as far as the respective size in the "Torpedo" type leads as there not as aerodynamic. To counter this, when casting longer distances, you may need to use a slightly heavier model than you would normally.

Whilst the Torpedo type leads are best for distance work, and the Pear leads for slopes, the Dumpy Multi Bomb and Dumpy Tri Bomb are the perfect all round models when range and holding power are not the deciding factor. The Dumpy shape is a combination of the Torpedo and Pear models and is a jack-of-all-trades lead that is very popular among our consultants. The Dumpy bombs have adequate holding power to be used on slopes up to 20 degrees and provide good resistance for "bolt" style rigs. In addition, they are aerodynamic enough to be cast fair distances.

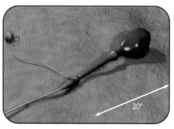

Finally we come to a real ground hog of a lead, the aptly named Kling On. This design is intended for situations that no other lead can cope with, namely fast

flowing rivers with plenty of current or smooth, steep slopes often associated with gravel bars and plateaux. The dimpled effect of the Kling On leads assures the user of maximum grip, at the same time imparting that all-important bolt effect so vital to many of today's modern bolt rigs. These leads are the direct descendants of the beach caster's watch lead a specially designed lead used to counter the strong cross currents that beach anglers commonly

encounter. However, carp anglers often find themselves in similar situations so Fox designed this lead to help them. The Kling On's flat profile tends to grip the riverbed in fast currents, such as the River Ebro pictured left, and prevents the lead being washed downstream. At the same time the lead's stubby design and extended dimples also prevent it from tumbling down a slope or the side

of a bar. Available in both in-line or pendant styles, the Kling On will prove itself time and time again in tricky situations.

# CHAPTER 6
# SNAG FISHING

## SNAG AND WEED FISHING

In Chapter 2 we discussed how weed beds, fallen trees and all other manner of snags act like magnets to carp. Carp adore these areas not only because they tend to hold food, but because they provide sanctuary and cover. It is not unusual to see carp that are normally cautious, feeding on boilies apparently without any suspicion whatsoever under the protection offered by these features.

For these reasons, Snag fishing is almost certainly going to play a part in most carp anglers fishing sooner or later, but is not to be undertaken lightly. Consideration for the carp should be at the forefront of all our minds when snag fishing and if you have any reservations at all, then don't do it. However, if done properly and common sense is applied, snag fishing can be exciting and very rewarding. Fox consultant, Frank Warwick, has had more than his fair share of success catching fish in snaggy conditions from waters throughout Europe. Here, Frank is pictured with a 40lb plus Mirror caught from a Belgium stillwater cluttered with weed.

In the following chapter, Frank Warwick outlines his approach to Snag Fishing and gives an insight into how to tackle weed in its various forms, lily pads and other potential problem situations.

## PREPERATION

Carp will always visit snags in their various forms. They seem to love the feeling of security and treat such places as a retreat where they can hide away from pressure. I have observed many times, from overhanging vantage points, carp feed excitedly in amongst a tangle of roots or underwater obstructions, whilst the carp in open water appeared to be completely off their feed. On many occasions when I've experienced this, the anglers fishing in open water swims who were having little or no action tended to put this down to the fact that, the carp simply "were not feeding". If this sounds familiar or if you are struggling to catch from open water, then now is definitely a good time to investigate the snags on your local water.

Before I commence fishing on any water I try to make it my business to have a good look in any snags, weed beds or lily pads to try and locate feeding fish. If you are lucky enough to find carp in residence, straight away, then of course the job is made instantly easier. However, one other point I should make is never be too hasty when fish spotting. On many occasions I have arrived and found snags devoid of carp only to have them arrive in numbers quite some time later. Quite often carp will come and go all day long, so a quick whistle stop fish spotting session could be deceiving. I tend to spend as much as half an hour at a time spotting fish in trees and bushes. I like to give the carp a chance to arrive, many a time I have only got down from vantage points because the soles of my feet were hurting from the pressure of continually standing on a branch.

One piece of equipment that is invaluable for fish spotting is a pair of Polaroid Sunglasses. Polaroid glasses, such as the Fox Series 300's, have lenses which selectively absorb light from one plane, reducing the surface glare, giving a clearer view of what is happening under the water.

Of course some snags don't always have a suitable fish spotting location and the water may be too coloured or too deep to see into clearly, but carp will spend at least some of their time visiting such places. Whenever I'm fishing close to snags particularly on a new water which I am not familiar with, I will first of all cast a lead (minus a hook and hooklength) around to feel for underwater obstacles. When doing so I start some distance from the main snag and gradually work my way closer, casting in a fan pattern to cover the main playing area and reveal any unforeseen problems. The last thing you want to do is to find out the hard way that the swim contains a lot more snags than you bargained for when playing a carp.

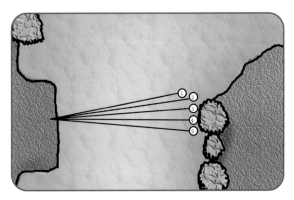

Another good reason for casting a lead around the swim is to locate other potential hazards like lost tackle. Unfortunately, tackle losses by other anglers are an unwanted by-product of fishing close to snags. Even if you know the swim well, there's always a chance that other anglers have been in the swim since your last visit and have lost terminal tackle, which might not be visible. Luckily most clubs, syndicates and water owners are safety minded these days and will generally check for lost tackle with a boat, but regardless of this check for yourself with a lead on a rod first.

During the time I spend casting around the swim there are a number of other things I like to take into account. Firstly, I weigh up the best possible position for playing the carp, once hooked. I take into consideration things like "can the fish kite sideways and clip anything, has the swim got enough room to play carp efficiently?" Quite often, the only way you can stop a carp, realistically, is to walk backwards whilst applying as much pressure as the tackle will take.

Another possibly obvious point is making sure the position you choose has sufficient room to make accurate casts. Once again this is of prime importance if success is to be had and is best determined prior to introducing bait and attempting to commence fishing. When fishing in the confines of a tight swim, it is sometimes better to kneel when casting to give yourself a little extra space.

## CASTING TO SNAGS

After leading around the swim you will hopefully have found out all the information you need; whether overhanging bushes are undercut or not, whether you can cast effectively, whether there are any unseen underwater obstructions. Assuming the answer to all these questions is "yes", the next factor is getting your rig and bait close to the snags or weed in question. This is tremendously important as I have certainly found the tighter I fish to a feature, the better the chance of a pick-up. Usually "near enough" is not enough, you have to really be on top of your accuracy to get the best from snag fishing.

I would strongly suggest − regardless of how experienced you are − having a few practice casts into open water with the rod and lead you intend to use, but don't attach a rig until you are happy you have the "feel" or measure of the cast.

There are two ways you can approach casting to snags. The first is to rely entirely on your own accuracy, fine for the skilled caster, but you run the risk of loosing your rig and lead. If you are at all unsure about casting, I would strongly advise you to use the line clip method I am about to describe.

1. First of all, cast as near as you can to the intended target, but ensure your lead lands short of the snags.

2. Take note of the position where you are standing/kneeling. This is important as you will need to stand in exactly the same place for all subsequent casts to ensure constant repetition.

3. If the cast falls fairly near the intended target, for example, say you were around 10ft short, then gently tighten up to the lead and pay out perhaps 5ft of line then put your line in the clip on the spool of your reel.

4. Repeat steps one and two getting gradually closer to the snag as you go along.

You may say "why not pass out 8ft or 9ft after the first cast and drop right near the target?" I would suggest that it is very easy to get carried away, over estimate the distance, and end up in the snags with your next cast. I find it far better to make a few extra casts letting out small amounts of line each time and using the line clip as a brake.

One thing I would point out is, if the mainline is tight to the clip as the lead enters the water, the rig is liable to recoil and bounce back towards the angler. One way to overcome this is to hold the rod at approximately 90 degrees to the water (pointing in the air) as the lead hits the water. As the lead falls through the water follow it with your rod tip which will stop the lead arcing away from the snag.

Another way to get a bait tight to snags, under an overhanging bush for instance, is to dispatch with the line clip and use a simple free flowing cast, relying solely on your own casting ability to hit the spot. The end result is the momentum of the lead will carry the baited rig as much as 5ft under an overhanging vegetation, so achieving a much better resting place where carp are more inclined to consider a bait "safe" and feed.

I remember after using a free flowing accuracy cast in the past, seeing lines of bubbles rise to the surface in tight undercut safe areas, where the momentum of the lead had disturbed the underlying silt. Quite often I was surprised at just how far a lead could travel especially a 4oz or 5oz lead. Nowadays, I always place a piece of the dissolving Fox Hi Riser foam on my hooks before casting. After being in the water for a short time, the Hi Riser foam floats to the surface so you can be sure of your rigs final resting position. It also has another superb property, it protects and masks the hook and certainly helps prevent the rig foam from gripping and catching on any foliage as the rig hits the area close to such hazardous stuff.

On one memorable session, I had to fish to snags to catch a carp for the making of a video. I knew that carp were hardly likely to be lured into feeding on the outer edges of the snags as it was obvious that almost every angler who would have fished this swim previously, would have positioned a bait here. It seemed to me, that in order to be fairly sure of a take, I would have to fish in a more extreme fashion.

A few good casts from a spare rod with only a lead on revealed that there were no serious snags under the overhanging canopy of branches; in fact it was remarkably clean under there. The main problem was the overhanging branches came to within 18 inches of the waters surface, so I would have virtually no room for error when casting. Clipping up was out of the question as this would never allow me to propel the lead right under the overhanging bushes, it would bounce back as mentioned previously, defeating the object. An accurate cast was my only option. Although the cast was not a great distance, perhaps 45 yards, I purposefully choose a heavy 5oz lead knowing that this would achieve maximum forward momentum.

This enabled me to use another ploy which I would advise you to try if you are casting under a low target. This is to kneel down when casting, it seriously changes the angle of the flight of the lead, and it makes even the most precarious cast far more likely to succeed. Another advantage is, that by kneeling down you also remain steadier on the cast.

Anyway, I managed to get two very good casts extremely tight under that overhanging bush and to be quite honest I could scarcely believe just how far those leads and rigs travelled underwater, as when the PVA foam rose to the surface it was literally no more than 5 or 6 inches from the bank and I would say nearly 6ft under the tree branches, perhaps more. That extreme type of casting caught me 3 carp on that occasion 25lbs, 34lbs and 41.6lbs very pleasant indeed! Getting baits in the right position is only part of the jigsaw, how to contain and diffuse a carps explosive power is crucially important and this is the next thing to consider.

Once you have taken all these steps its then down to how accurate you are. To be quite honest, you need to have a bit of bottle at times and know when and when not to slow the flight of the lead and rig down by tapping the tip of your reels spool a couple of times just before the lead hits the target. As with anything, practice makes perfect, which will give you the confidence needed for good accurate casting.

Before I go into detail about the rigs I use, there is one important piece of advice I want to give to anyone fishing near snags and for that matter weed – LOSE THE LEAD. Most problems occur when the lead is pulled through underwater obstacles such as branches, weed or lilies. If your lead is discharged from the rig, soon after a take, the hooked carp will usually rise to the surface and you will be in direct contact, so the odds of landing the fish will fall heavily in your favour.

To ensure my leads release quickly, I trim down my safety clips and tail rubbers, so at the merest hint of pressure, the lead will drop off. You may ask "what about the loss of a lead? They are expensive!" Firstly, if you take into account the time and effort we put into catching carp the price of a lead is insignificant.

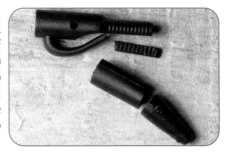

Secondly, if you don't drop the lead you may well loose all your tackle and the carp!

I recently fished a large water in Belgium where a massive explosion of weed, had colonised the whole of the lake in less than 18 months. I knew the carp favoured the deep far margins which involved fishing at long range. I did not think twice about fishing drop off leads, it was simply essential, both from an indication and playing carp point of view. My plan worked well and during the night I caught a number of carp, each of which gave a good indication. Without a lead in the way, the carp were also easy to land as my terminal tackle avoided the usual giant ball of weed, which could have reached 30lb in weight, making the job a nightmare.

One of my Belgium colleagues commented that he had a series of bleeps throughout the night, which he attributed to bream, on one of his rods. When I asked "are you fishing drop off leads", he said "no way, they are too much money to simply loose". When we went out in the boat to unhook the expected Bream and clear the usual giant weed ball, my colleague was shocked to find a very angry 47lb scaled mirror amongst the resultant mess. Quite simply, the carp had picked up his bait then run a short distance sometime during the night, and the lead had obviously become locked up solid in the mass of weed. Unable to move, the carp had simply sat there all night. Had the line broke at any point, that carp would very probably never have broken free. I think this story illustrates just how important the lead set-up is in both success and carp welfare.

The rig I use for most of my snag fishing isn't overly complicated. My reel line tends to consist of 15lb Soft Steel, I only resort to 20lb in severe conditions. If sharp muscle clad branches are expected, or I'm fishing at range, I'll substitute Soft Steel for 32lb Submerge Braid. To tie the rest of the rig you will need:- Size 4 (or 6) Series 2XS hooks, 25lb Insider, Barbuster Rig Tube, Carp Safety Clips, 1mm Silicone Tube, Clear Shrink Tube and some Anti-Tangle Sleeves.

## SNAG RIG

1. First tie a Series 2XS to a 20cm length of Insider with a knotless knot, then remove 4cm of the coating.

2. Thread a 15mm piece of clear shrink tube over the hook length and shrink over the eye of the hook.

3. Cut down your safety lead clip and rubber sleeve if you haven't already done so.

4. Thread your nylon mainline through a 20cm length of 0.75mm Barbuster Tube and safety lead clip before tying to the swivel with a Grinner knot.

5. Thread the Anti Tangle Sleeve up the Insider before tying the hook length to the swivel with a Grinner knot.

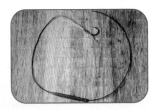

**5** Slide the anti-tangle sleeve back over the swivel to protect the knot and prevent tangles during casting.

**6** Position your bait on the hair before placing the lead on the leg of the clip and secure by pushing the tail rubber in to place.

**7** Place a piece of Hi Riser foam on the point of the hook prior to casting to protect the hook from debris and pinpoint the position of the rig.

When using this rig I like to use a comparatively heavy lead. This allows me to fish "locked up" solid, with a tight line between the lead and rod tip, which in turn gives a positive indication. I have experimented with lighter leads in the past and found the delay between the take and indication gives the carp too much time to pick up speed and power their way into snags.

For heavy duty snag and weed fishing I think that strong, short shanked, beak point hooks such as the Fox Series 2XS are vital. This style of hook tend to bed in during the fight and are far less prone to slipping out in "hit and hold" situations.

### Weed Rigs

Certain types of weed can be very abrasive indeed and I think braid can be advantageous in this situation. Braid has a tendency to cut through weed like a knife through butter, whereas nylon will grate and become easily damaged. If you do use nylon mainline in weedy water, choose one with a high degree of abrasion resistance like Fox Barbuster, and always feel for damage when winding in.

The rig I use for Weed fishing is almost identical to the one I use for Snag fishing. The components used are identical but because threading braid through thin anti tangle tubing can be a nightmare, I replace the 0.75mm tubing with 45lb lead core.

## WEED RIG

1. Follow steps 1 to 3 from the Snag rig then take a length of 45lb lead core with a swivel spliced into one end and a loop in the other. Earlier in the book we covered making lead core leaders. Alternatively use a ready-made Fox Lead Core Anti-Tangle Rig.

2. Thread the cut down lead clip and tail rubber on to the lead core before attaching your mainline to the loop in the lead core.

3. Thread an Anti-Tangle sleeve up your hook length before tying the Insider to the swivel with a Grinner knot. Slide the sleeve backwards to protect the knot and prevent tangles when the rig is in flight.

Up until now, with the exception of the addition of the lead core, the rig looks very much the same. However, this is where things start to get different.

4. Using 6lb mono, such as Fox Soft Steel, tie a loop to the eye of the lead, before placing over the leg of the line clip. (We've used Magic Marker in this illustration).

5. Finally, add your bait/baits and a piece of Hi-Riser foam and you are ready to go.

The nylon provides a weak link which will definitely break away should the lead hit weed, pads or a snag. Should a take not occur you can still retrieve your lead and recast without a problem. When casting long distances, to provide an additional means of security, I tie the lead to the clip with some PVA string.

## TACKLE SET UP

In my experience if you hook a carp near snags and let the fish run, you'll have problems. In doing so, you let the carp build up speed and momentum and usually in these situations there's only one thing on the carps mind, to plough through as many underwater features as it can in as short a space of time. The result, more often than not, ends with the angler being cut off or snagged solid.

The only reliable solution is to fish 'locked up solid'. By this I mean, literally that the set is virtually bullet proof, with goal post buzzer bars and bank sticks pushed into the bank in place of a pod. One bank stick — even if used with a stabilizer — is not enough to resist a powerful take from a carp as they will twist a single bank stick easily which can result in the angler losing a rod and reel.

I always fish with the butt ring of the rod firmly butted up behind my Microns and secure the rod butts in place with Duo Grip Rod Rests. Without a "rod lock" style rod rest there is still a chance, in an extreme situation, that the butt ring can fight its way over the Micron. I have a friend, Paul Hunt, who had a carp on Pit 1 Elstow give such a powerful take, that his butt ring hit the buzzer and snapped the ears of the buzzer clean off in an instant; frightening power".

I also have my reel clutches screwed down tight so no line whatsoever can be taken from the reel. If you use a freespool type reel make sure this mechanism is also set on its maximum setting.

On the indicator front I use Swingers or Springers. Whichever type you choose, make sure the arm is loaded with plenty of weight and is set tight. Doing this will give you the best possible warning of an impending take. You should always sit right next to your rods; when i get a take I am on the rod like a flash. I am prepared to use a tight line and risk spooking the occasional carp, in order to avoid giving carp the time to gather momentum, which could happen with a slacker line drop arm indicator.

As soon as I hook a fish I will play the carp firmly, and if possible walk quickly backwards, to get the carp into open water. Pressure can be applied quickly and more effectively walking backwards than by solely pumping the carp with the rod and reel. Combine the two together and you will stop even the most powerful of carp before it has a chance to get up a head of steam.

I often fish with rods at right angles to the snags. By using heavy leads of 4 or 5 ounces I am able to tighten down to the leads so that they're on the point of being dislodged, and the whole of the rod is bent around like a giant sprung quiver tip. By using this method, when a carp is hooked the lead is immediately dislodged and the rod starts applying pressure and even spring backs. The result is often a shocked carp giving a dramatic drop back, usually kiting in a semi circle away from danger. The only problem with this system is it only works if you are fishing side on to snags.

If you are fishing directly at snags then I would advise you to point the rod tips directly at the target. This removes any chance of the rods being pulled off the buzzer, which can happen if your lines are at an angle to the rod tip and you don't re-enforce the set up with extra bank sticks, as I have shown in the previous diagram.

I have seen anglers fishing towards snags with their rods pointing towards their leads but with the tips high in the air, continental style. With monfilament mainline, in particular, the stretch in the nylon and the give in the rod combine to give the carp just enough slack to gather pace. I have witnessed some crazy sights of rod tips suddenly slamming over forcing the rod butt from the rear rod rest and the rod suddenly cannoning into the lake, all in seconds. For this reason, I think it best to point the rod directly at the lead with rods kept low and parallel to the water. Braided mainline is an excellent aid when quick decision is so vital and, of course, its lack of stretch allows you much more instant control.

## Conclusion

I don't believe Snag fishing is any more difficult than any other type of fishing, providing you follow the basic guide lines I've laid down. As I mentioned at the start of the chapter, fishing close to weed and snags can be highly productive and is a technique every angler should learn. Always remember, fish safety is paramount and as with all types fishing, time spent preparing will pay dividends in the future.

# CHAPTER 7
# CARING FOR
# YOUR CATCH

Carp care is the number one priority for Fox International, and rightly so. As more and more anglers join the ranks, carp fishing is now the most popular and widely practised form of angling in the UK. As a result, our precious quarry is under increasing pressure and it is beholden to us, as a leading company in the big fish world, to ensure we do everything possible to look after them while they are in our care.

Fox are not alone. Nowadays, carp care has become a higher and higher priority and all the tackle firms put great stress on making sure the carp are looked after as gently as possible while out of the water.

The time a carp can spend out of the water can vary according to the water temperature, believe it or not. In winter, the lake water carries a great deal more oxygen than in summer, so it follows that it is even more important to minimise the time the fish is on the bank during the summer months.

If your camera is not set up, or if there is nobody immediately close by to take your photos, it is best to pop the fish in a sack for a few minutes. Alternatively, unhook the fish and leave it in the net. Make sure the net is secured to the bank and that the net cord is above the water!

## Weighing fish

If the fish appears to have fully recovered and is looking pretty lively, allow the fish to rest on its side **(never on its belly)** in the sack, for a couple of minutes. This will give the carp's eyes time to adjust to the light and will also calm it down. Next, allow the fish to get used to full daylight by

opening the sack close to its head so that the eye is uncovered. Have the sack ready to drape across the fish's head again if it starts to flap. If a fish is going to start kicking up, it's most likely to do so when daylight hits its eye.

Gradually expose the head to daylight until the fish has adjusted to the change from the blackness of the sack to the brightness of the daylight.

After taking these steps you should find that the fish will be far less likely to flap about, allowing you to do the photos quickly and with the minimum of risk to the fish.

You might say that keeping it out of the water for a couple of minutes is damaging to the fish, but it is not half as damaging as the fish flapping about in your arms, falling to the ground, missing the mat and ending up dead or injured. You can minimise the risk of damage to a fish by using a decent weighing sling. The Fox Safety Weigh Sling is one of the best designs available. It is made of PVC coated nylon, which makes it very slippery when wet and it protects carp from damaging mucus loss. It has two sections of web netting sewn in at the lower corners that allow water to escape quickly giving a reliable, accurate weight reading.

Incidentally, the Sling can also be used as a five-minute sack. Simply zip up the two end zips and twist the handles together. Then push a bankstick through the small gap formed between the handles and push the bankstick into the lakebed or close to the margin so the Sling is immersed. The fish will be held trapped between the sides of the Sling while you get the camera set up.

Finally, the Safety Weigh Sling has solid reinforcing bars to strengthen the Sling and prevent it from folding itself around the fish. This encourages the fish to lie straight and flat and on its side (very important) in the bottom of the Sling while being weighed.

The Sling also features a pair of zips that run along the edges. These ensure that the fish is held securely and safely which you carry it back to the water's edge.

Here is our recommended way of handling a fish using the Safety Weigh Sling.

- Place the dampened Weigh Sling on your unhooking mat.

- Place the fish, still in the landing net, on the opened Sling.

- Unhook the fish.

- Transfer the fish from the landing net to the Sling.

- Zip up the two sides.

- Weigh the fish

- Once weighed, take the fish back to the unhookng mat before taking photos. It is worth having a tub of water alongside the mat to pour over the fish prior to taking pictures.

- After you've taken pictures, return the fish to the Safety Weigh sling. Keep the fish over the unhooking mat at all times in case it flaps at any time.

- Once the fish is in the Safety Weigh Sling it can be carried back to the water using the soft touch neoprene carry handles. (Make sure both ends of the Sling are zipped). Flood the sling with water.

- At this point it is worth leaving the fish to rest for a couple of minutes to get its breath back.

- Hold the Sling upright and unzip the end of the sling from which you wish to release the fish – ideally this should be the end where the carp's head is resting.

- The fish will make its own mind up when it is ready to swim off and it invariably does so with little or no fuss whatsoever.

### Sacking Fish

Even though it may be banned on some lakes, it can actually benefit the fish if it is sacked up for a few minutes as it gives it time to rest and recover. There is nothing wrong with sacking a fish as long as it is done sensibly in a well-designed sack. The Fox Carp Sack is made of very heavy-duty material with a strong zip fastener and two carrying handles to ensure that the fish is not harmed in any way during its period in the sack. The material is made of a fairly open weave material that allows for good water exchange and it also features and extra long, heavy-duty cord and bankstick clip.

Whichever Carp Sack you choose to use, it is important you adhere to the following guidelines when sacking fish to ensure their safety:

Always ensure that there is plenty of deep water in the area where you sack the fish.

Never sack a fish in shallow water, especially during the summer months. In summer, the margins can heat up very quickly and as they do so the water looses oxygen and a sacked fish could easily die of suffocation.

Similarly, never sack a fish in a spot where the sack might become enveloped in silt. Again, the risk of suffocation is very real if the sack sinks into deep silt.

Try to ensure that you only sack a fish where the lakebed is hard. A small amount of silt is acceptable, but deep silt can be dangerous.

It is imperative that the bankstick, the Carp Sack is secured to, is pushed securely in to the ground: THE FISH'S LIFE DEPENDS ON THIS. Banksticks with a screw thread such as the Fox Powerpoint models offer an extra degree of security in these circumstances.

Once the fish is in the sack pay out enough of the thread to allow the fish to sit up in even deeper water. Whilst all of the above points are essential when sacking fish, the golden rule is "Never sack a fish for longer than is absolutely necessary". A carp can recover its strength remarkably quickly and even if left in the sack for as little as twenty minutes it will have got its breath back by the time you come to do the photos. As a result, you can end up going fifteen rounds with a very lively and angry fish which puts it at risk, and often results in some pretty useless photos as you end up soaked in sweat and covered in slime.

# Index:

# Index cont.

# Index cont.

## N, O.

## P, Q.

## R.

## S.